GLOBAL CIVILIZATION

Cross Cultural Theologies

Series Editors: Jione Havea and Clive Pearson, United Theological College, Sydney and Charles Sturt University, New South Wales, Australia

This series focuses on how the "cultural turn" in interdisciplinary studies has informed theology and biblical studies. It takes its leave from the experience of the flow of people from one part of the world to another.

It moves beyond the crossing of cultures in a narrow diasporic sense. It will entertain perspectives that arise out of generational criticism, gender, sexual orientation, and the relationship of art and film to theology. It will explore the sometimes competing rhetoric of multiculturalism and cross-culturalism and will demonstrate a concern for the intersection of globalization and how those global flows of peoples and ideas are received and interpreted in localized settings. The series will seek to make use of a range of disciplines including the study of cross-cultural liturgy, travel, the practice of ministry and worship in multi-ethnic locations and how theologies that have arisen in one part of the world have migrated to a new location. It will look at the public nature of faith in complex, multicultural, multireligious societies and compares how diverse faiths and their theologies have responded to the same issues.

The series welcomes contributions by scholars from around the world. It will include both single-authored and multi-authored volumes.

Forthcoming in the series:

Bibles and Baedekers: Tourism, Travel, Exile and God
Michael Grimshaw

Black Religion and Black Theology in Britain: A Reader
Edited by: Michael N. Jagessar and Anthony G. Reddie

GLOBAL CIVILIZATION
CHALLENGES TO SOCIETY AND TO CHRISTIANITY

Leonardo Boff

Translated by Alexandre Guilherme

LONDON   OAKVILLE

Published by

UK: Equinox Publishing Ltd
Unit 6, The Village,
101 Amies St.,
London, SW11 2JW

US: DBBC,
28 Main Street,
Oakville, CT 06779

www.equinoxpub.com

First published in Portuguese in 2003 by Animus/Anima Producoes titled *Nova Era: A Civilização Planetária*
First published in English 2005 by Equinox Publishing Ltd.

British Library Cataloguing-in-Publication Data
A catalogue record for this book is available from the British Library.

Library of Congress Cataloging-in-Publication Data

Boff, Leonardo.
  [Nova era. English]
  Global civilization : challenges to society and to Christianity /
Leonardo Boff ; translated by Alexandre Guilherme.
      p. cm. -- (Cross cultural theologies)
  Translation of: Nova era : a civilização planetária : desafios à
sociedade e ao cristianismo
  Includes bibliographical references and index.
  ISBN 1-84553-004-7 (hb) -- ISBN 1-84553-005-5 (pb)
  1. Social history--1970- 2. Liberation theology. I. Title. II.
Series.
  HN18.B58313 2005
  261--dc22
                                  2004029418

ISBN   1 84553 004 7   (hardback)
ISBN   1 84553 005 5   (paperback)

Typeset by CA Typesetting, www.sheffieldtypesetting.com
Printed and bound in Great Britain by Antony Rowe Ltd, Eastbourne

Contents

Chapter 10
How Much does Christianity Help with the
Construction of the 21st Century?

Chapter 11
Conclusion to Part II: We are all Eagles

Part III
Conclusion

Chapter 12
Recreating a Utopic Horizon

Appendix A: Earth's Charter

Appendix B: The Ages of Globalization

Appendix C: The Globalization Process and its Challenges
to Liberation Theology

Preface

The language of globalization has increasingly become a part of a common intellectual agenda over the last couple of decades. It is a term that sometimes operates in an umbrella fashion, providing shelter for a range of theories to do with economics, cultural consciousness, politics, informational technology and a whole raft of global ethical flows to do with justice, citizenship, accountability, care of the environment and the like. Its definition is far from settled and is susceptible to a range of nuances. Those who write in the field invariably feel obliged to offer yet another working definition to capture this emerging sense of an interrelated one world, shaped by a compression of time and place.

The frequent employment of this protean label is relatively recent: word watchers can look back to its first recorded usage, maybe in 1944. This was a period in which there was a widening use of terms such as global attitudes and, unfortunately, global warfare. In the more fully fledged form of globalization it seems to have begun to insinuate itself increasingly into the way we speak about the world from the early 1960s. Its present popularity is even more recent and perhaps is tied to the collapse of the Berlin Wall and the bipolar politics of the Cold War. Its ready usage has arguably seen the relative demise of the once commonly invoked description of some countries and economies being Third World. That designation does seem to feature less these days and perhaps the word globalization is symptomatic of a deep-seated, paradigmatic change in which we find ourselves.

In terms of linguistic history, then, globalization is a newcomer to human discourse. The momentum which has led to its manifestation has been longer in the making. It is not uncommon to look back to the age of European expansion, for instance, and its legacy of imperialism and colonialism. Such a pre-history is a sign of how this term and the processes at work within this ethos are far from innocent. The very idea of a world culture or a global system does not commend itself to all. It can appear to be the product of elitism. It is forever running the risk of undermining the local and particular. In a theological conference I attended at Chiang Mai in northern Thailand, in August 2003, it was evident that globalization was not deemed to be a positive word. One speaker after another saw it as the equivalent of the new American empire and a form of neo-colonialism. The intersection of the global and the local is obviously a part of this dynamic. It should come as no surprise that the policies of globalization have spawned a complex set of strategies of resistance and accommodation. Maybe globalization should not be discussed apart from its parasitic derivative, glocalization.

This translation of Leonardo Boff's *Global Civilization* stands inside this ferment of ideas, values and practices. Its angle and theme is particular and closely linked to the contemporary discussion on whether or not there is a global civil society. What is of particular interest here is that Boff writes from a background in theology and Christian ethics. It is now recognized, of course, that globalization is also an important issue for these disciplines to address. There is an increasing number of research institutes and conferences on public theology dedicated to the exploration of globalization, in general, and global citizenship and civilization, more specifically. Into such an arena Boff emerges as a distinguished figure insofar as he has been one of the outstanding advocates of a liberation theology in Latin America and beyond. He has been to the fore in weaving together a concern for the poor and the earth. It is not that long ago since assorted international theological and ethical gatherings on the state of the environment could end up in an impasse because care for the environment was reckoned to be a luxury of the well-off world and perhaps a means of keeping the less developed world poor. Boff brought these two "wounds" together around the time of the Rio Earth Summit.

That Boff has been able to bring together concerns for the poor and ecology is in keeping with the emergence of his interest in a global civilization. This present brief text covers a much wider range of themes. It is a brave book in this respect, for it covers so much change and many disciplines in what is really just a handful of pages. Boff is able to do this because though there is an empirical, descriptive aspect to his work, there is something else as well. Permeating his writing is an almost mystical, sacramental sense that is straining to be prophetic. The simplicity of the actual text is deceptive as a result. It can mask a great deal of scholarship that lies embedded in the argument. The translation by Alexandre Guilherme has striven to respect as far as possible Boff's style and referencing.

This theme of global civilization might seem, at first glance, an odd selection for a series on cross-cultural theologies. The very idea of a global society can presuppose a desire for commonality and universality. It is likely to be a "big picture" approach. By way of comparison, the cross-cultural tendency is to notice difference, to dwell in liminal and threshold spaces, and be quite specific. And yet these two ways of looking at contemporary society — the global and the cross-cultural — are not antithetic. The prospect of a diasporic, cross-cultural theology is made possible by the global flows of people from one part of the world to the next. It is a facet of globalization to live alongside neighbors who come from so many nations and ethnicities. And, as for this particular thesis of a global civilization, Boff is writing from the perspective of "the great south." So often the discussion on globalization is North Atlantic-based. Boff is shifting hemispheres.

A text on global civilization belongs inside a series on cross-cultural theologies. The experience of globalization furnishes the dislocation and the opportunity for such work to be done. Leonardo Boff has been one of the great theologians of the latter quarter of the twentieth century; here we have a translation of a Portuguese text (2003) that is seeking to cross over into the first decades of the new millennium.

Clive Pearson
Sydney, February 2005

Introduction

The process of globalization that occurs through the economy, politics, militarism, techno-science, communication and spirituality is increasingly consolidating itself. With this fact emerges a new kind of consciousness of global proportions, a new kind of reasoning that embraces the complexities of reality and a new cosmology. This new cosmology brings with it the insight that the Earth is part of the cosmos, which is still evolving. The Earth when seen from the perspective of astronauts emerges as a blue and white planet; it does not appear as an inert ship, but as an enormous living organism. This is Gaia, a unique and diverse reality that is contradictory and complementary, and which is our common fatherland (father) and motherland (mother). Human beings, thus, understand themselves as sons and daughters of the Earth and the result of ancient forces and energies that have been acting in the universe for billions of years.

This unification requires a central nervous system. The means of communication, the inter-dependence of all, with all, everywhere and at every moment, the number of human beings that are conscious of the inter-retro-relations between everything, all these function as if they were neurons of the planet Earth. Are we moving towards the rise of a new collective consciousness, a noosphere, just as in the past the litho-sphere, the atmosphere, the biosphere and anthroposphere arose? Are we about to experience a new phenomenon in the cosmological process?

What will happen to the two-thirds of human beings, sons and daughters of the Earth, that find themselves marginalized in this global era?

What is the function of religions, particularly Christianity, in devising the very thing that connects and re-connects all phenomena; and that, in the religious sphere, deciphers the Sacred and the Mystery that are proclaimed within this emerging reality and that can unite and centralize all human experience?

What is the responsibility of each of us in bringing about deep changes that are synchronized with the wider picture of things?

For new music, new ears.

My thoughts in this book are new and tentative. This book is aimed to touch readers so that they can see the wider picture of things happening around them. It is aimed at helping the readers to unite themselves with the whole of humanity, helping in the creation of an Earth that is unified in sharing, in justice, in love and in peace.

Leonardo Boff
Rio de Janeiro, Easter 1994

Part I
The Rise of a New Global Civilization

A Perspective from the Great South

There is almost a consensus nowadays among world social analysts that we are currently going through great cultural changes as well as changes in civilization *per se*. We are entering a new phase for humankind, a new level of consciousness, and a new age for the planet Earth. These changes have impinged greatly on world religions, including Christianity, which aim to maintain and communicate a common message to all human beings and give a meaning to the universe.

Before critically assessing both the above premise and how the process of globalization impinges on Christianity, we must understand the phenomena and the logic behind this process. Globalization is occurring mainly on three fronts, namely, technological change, the globalization of the market forces, and the rise of a new global conscience. Let us now briefly assess each of these fronts which are shaping the new civilization.

1   The New Nature of Technological Progress

The Brazilian anthropologist Darcy Ribeiro (1968) demonstrated, in his great work *O Processo Civilatorio* (*The Civilizational Process*), that changes in societies begin with the introduction of new technologies, which change the dialogue between the society and the world and between the various agents of that same society. Without a doubt, we are currently living through an accelerated process of technological change. Let us now consider this in finer detail.

From the Neolithic Age to the 1950s, humankind knew and made use of two characteristics of matter, namely its mass and its energy. In particular, mass has been researched and used by the classical physics of Newton and Galileo since the 16th century. Energy became the object of much research during the 19th century and the beginning of the 20th century. Mass and energy, and more specifically electric and nuclear energy, enabled projects of industrialization and of technological advancement, which have created all kinds of devices that facilitate and improve living conditions.

Nature, however, contains another characteristic which up to now has been unexplored, namely *information*. All beings, alive or not, are the carriers of particular data that can be assessed, measured in bytes (*binary digit*), and stored in computers. This data is built into machines as commands and used by us in our daily life as we deal with domestic digital devices (such as TVs, telephones, computers and even washing machines) and seen by us in artificial communication satellites and space exploration ships.

Telecommunications, biotechnology (i.e. the DNA-RNA chain of the human genome, which contain all necessary information for the constitution of a human being), computer science and robotics technically express this new knowledge of reality that is information. Its application brings substantial advantages to calculations, to paradigms of natural phenomena and to many other applications; it is even used in the common motorcar.

This new reality has introduced a new alphabet, the computer science language. It has turned reality into an invisible and miniaturized entity. The consumption of energy used in computations is minimal. To access one byte of information costs only 10^{-16} of a degree of heat on the Kelvin scale. A new relation with time and space is also created. A laptop computer (small space) can make extremely complex calculations with extraordinary speed (little time) and, moreover, this is done with minimum consumption of energy (four batteries).

This has a direct impact on the social aspect of labor relations: there is a continuous non-recoverable reduction of the labor force and an increasing exclusion of human participation in the means of production.

We are currently implementing on a large scale an informational society that is increasingly automated. The economy has changed. The economy is no longer dominated by the shortage and rarity of commodities, but by the low-cost production of goods and services.

These changes are so great that they mean much more than a new industrial revolution within the current and conventional paradigm of development, as argued by A. Toffler in his book *The Third Wave*. It certainly is this but much more, since it is a complete turn in history as it discharges key-concepts in the building and understanding of societies and of the evolutionary process and of the meaning of our passage through this Universe.

For instance, informatics enables a great quantitative rise in production without the generation of jobs, and, in some cases, it even destroy jobs in important sectors of manufacturing, agriculture, and services. Informatics increasingly does away with human labor.

From a Society of Full Employment to a Society of Maximum Activity

Up to recent times all production and a great part of culture were based on human labor. National constitutions emphasize the importance of labor. In paragraph 23 of the Universal Declaration of Human Rights it is stated that "everyone has the right to work, to free choice of employment, to just and favorable conditions of work and to protection against unemployment." Labor emerged thus, both to capitalism and to socialism, as the building force of the world and culture, as a fundamental human right, as the enabling force of human self-development and as the shaper of human destiny. Unemployment, in the classical society, was viewed as a momentary glitch. The ideal aimed at by every society was to enable full employment for all members of society. It was inadmissible to comprehend and accept unemployment as a normal consequence of a technological revolution. Everything was set in place to provide employment for everybody. This is exactly the opposite of our current state of affairs. The computerized and roboticized productive system produces more and better with almost no human labor input. Production of goods currently exceeds the developed world's needs. The connection between production and necessity has been dissolved. The point is never to cease increasing production. It follows from this that the idea of need must be aroused in people, even if artificially, so that these needs can be met by an ever increasing production.

At a closer look, however, the issue is not crucially centered at the production level, but in market control. To produce is relatively easy. The difficulty is selling the produce. This is the reason why companies must create a market for their produce, thus the importance and priority of marketing communication during the manufacturing process. It is the marketing communication that brings market dominance through the arousal of needs in consumers and which direct these consumers to products launched on the market in their urge to satisfy those needs. The media sector is by far the most dynamic in this cultural revolution that manifests itself in mass media, marketing, and so-called cultural goods, such as cinema films, music, photography, interior design, product design, fashion, tourism, sport, leisure activities, concerts, educational courses and games. Even food has transformed itself into a kind of communication in the form of pizza places, barbecue places, self-service restaurants, hamburgers, and the McDonald's and Bob's chains and the soft drink Coke.

Thus, the intensive use of technological information generates a structural unemployment. This is the great problem faced by all countries in the world, even developing countries, since even these bring in new technologies in their production lines.

Breaking free from the necessity of working under tiring, repetitive, deteriorating and dehumanizing conditions has been a long-sought-after dream. There was a longing for the freedom of creation, of enjoyment and auto-production without coercive limitations. In this kind of scenario one speaks of leisurely creation and of emancipated work. Our current means of production, however, exclude many people from the labor market. Following this exclusion, there is a social exclusion and a feeling of awkwardness that may lead to a feeling of shame.

The high unemployment rates experienced in the developed countries are structural and permanent and are, by and large, the outcome of this new phase of human society.

Between 1970 and 1990, and maintaining the same levels thereafter, unemployment in Europe went from 2.4 million to 16 million (10 percent of the economically active population). The poor of Europe currently number more than 50 million people. In the USA this figure is about 35 million.

Informatics and robotics, added to the unequal relations in international trade, which favor the developed countries to the detriment of the developing countries, created this amazing phenomena: in the last 30 years Europe has increased its wealth threefold and at the same time managed to diminish working hours by a quarter.

While there is an increase in the amount of goods and services produced through technological advancements, there is also an increase in the number of people excluded from the labor market, and also of the socially excluded. Jacques Robin, director of Transversales, Science et Culture de Paris, noted well that "The history of applied technology can be described on one hand as the improvement of living standards, and on the other hand as the succession of two kinds of poverty: dire poverty and unemployment; the first comes from work, the second from the lack of work."[1]

This situation only aggravates things further, since the benefits achieved through these technological advancements are not socialized, and thus they do not benefit the whole of the population, being reinvested in new, more advanced technologies so that companies can strengthen their position in the market, face their competitors, and produce even more.

This kind of paradigm based on technological development prolongs the perversity of the current capitalist model of development since it supports (1) a primacy of quantity over quality, (2) a privileged position for capital and the means of production over the labor force, and (3) a predominance of the material over the humanistic, the ethical and the spiritual.

Reality is Image

We are currently experiencing a new kind of technical development, which brings with it new kinds of social relations. The basis of social relations is no longer labor, but communication and informatics.

There is a new element encompassing this new emerging civilization: the image, which is an offspring of informatics. José Comblin, the liberation theologian who lives in Brazil and a keen observer of global trends, expressed this well when he wrote:

> Nowadays we are seeing the emergence of a new understanding of "living." The role of a person in society, or better said, the role of a person in the "theater of society" is more important than her labor. It is due to this fact that social activities, acting, leisure, concerts, and exhibiting are so important. For a businessman, the interviews given to the media are more important than his labor. Labor is a way of accessing a certain social status, which is now a performance. Labor does not have an intrinsic value anymore, its value relies on the kind of social performance that it enables. Insofar as labor is concerned it is not important what it can produce but the prestige that it can bring, and the way it can make a subject standout in society.[2]

In this changing society, the individual's self-realization is the main concern. This self-realization does not always come from that person's labor, as it can be realized through different kinds of activities, and alternative and autonomous occupations, such as opening a small hotel that targets ecologically conscious people as its customers, or satisfying personal hobbies or interests such as visiting historical places in a particular region or going for walks in a national park, and so on. Thus, one can see the importance nowadays of leisure time and of holidays (which is the central focus for those who work the whole year). The free weekend is far more important than the rest of the other working days.

Even life in society has changed. Before, one experienced society through active participation. This was the so-called active citizenship. Nowadays, however, one experiences society through the means of communication. We know what is happening in the places we live through what is aired by the radio and television stations and written by the newspapers. The city has become a great stage through its shopping malls, shopping windows, matches, and concerts. Everything has become a mass media image. Whatever has not been shown on the TV does not exist, did not happen. This is a global show with Olympic Games, international football championships, show-business, and great singers such as Pavarotti, Carreras, Elton John, and The Beatles; it extends itself even further as armed conflicts and wars, such as the two wars against Iraq, which were primarily a media and technological conflict. Everybody was able to take part in the battles by way of their TV sets, and, with certain tranquillity, support one side or the other as if watching a sports match.

Everybody has become a spectator and has the desire to be one. It is through images that the citizen contemplates him or herself and is able to project his or her own personal identity into society. Our individual personal identity is increasingly the projection of our own particular image in society. It now has less to do with one's inner self, the dialogue that lies within, and how we mediate the inner and external worlds we inhabit. One either takes part in this world-show in a direct manner, as participant actor, or indirectly through imagination and images. José Comblin noted that the mass does not practice sport, but watches it on TV; the mass does not produce music, but listens to it; the mass does not make history, but talks about it. It is through images that the mass feels that it is taking part in history and not being excluded from it. The masses are, however, passive participants, mere consumers and not active citizens, who manifest their opinions, who criticize, and who refuse to support certain views and conscientiously defend certain causes.

Such changes in society have transformed the old traditional idea of fighting for workers' rights. The worker has lost status. However, it must be said that there are workers who know much more than their bosses. These workers deal with a large amount of information and knowledge, and this gives them more actual power than the actual owner of the company. The businessperson is a mere specialist in *management*; he or she is one of the workers, so to speak; he or she does not, however, renounce his or her privileged position as the owner of the company and the right of accumulation that comes with it. In order to guarantee the continuation of their employment, workers team up with the companies they work for, producing a team effort in an attempt to fence off competitors. Instead of the class war, we have now the war between companies. The company that does not hold its ground in such a competitive market succumbs and ends up being swallowed by better positioned companies. The worker, fearing unemployment, prefers to accept, even if unwillingly, to support the company she works for, even if the company exploits her, because the company guarantees her employment and some sort of activity; and thus, this situation guarantees the employee a proper place in society and an active position in her family.

We are now seeing the beginning of the post-television era, as a revolution with numerical, synthetic and virtual images takes place. Thanks to numerical synthesis (no longer the 0, 1 binary system, but the 16 to 64 multiple system – for now) and to mathematical models in computers, we are now able to create images that feel more real than the ones produced by photography. Moreover, unlike photography and filming, there is no need for an actual reality as a basis. It is possible to create simulations that give a visible and realistic form to abstract ideas and daring dreams. This technology enables a cloning (the creation of a perfect double) of people and objects. Through the cloning of a human representation it is possible to create scenarios that project a new form of reality. For instance, the image of a Benedictine monk from Monte Carlo has been cloned as a guide to the Museum of Cluny (a place in the South-east of France where the great Benedictine reform of the 11th and 12th centuries took place), which is in Paris. Both the cloned representation and the real monk guide tourists through the museum and comment on it. Everything, however, is nothing more than a synthesis of images.

One must not forget also virtual images. Thanks to visual stereoscopic techniques, spectators feel themselves immersed in the image, taking part in this imaginary world that unfolds around them from all sides and angles. Technology in this area is being developed so that TV sets (called 3D TV) produce visual stereographic effects that enable the spectator to "enter" into the image. A laser of low intensity can produce images in the back of the eye; the laser beam excites the optical nerve, doing away with the necessity of real images and TV screens. This is the beginning of the so-called "cyberspace era." Visual imaging enables a new form of tele-presence and tele-work (e.g. teleconference and videoconference). Obviously, such technology also has a military use. It is able to simulate battles in virtual set-ups with very fine details that would not be possible should the simulated battles take place in factual reality. (This kind of technology was used during the Gulf War of 1991 through a Pentagon computer program called SAKI, and it was used again in the second Gulf War of 2003 when practically all infrastructure in Iraq was destroyed.)

With the so-called "electronic highways" a new system of writing and literacy emerges, that is, a writing revolution is taking place. There is a new alphabet in this neo-reality that runs along with the factual-reality. This neo-reality enables a very efficient manipulation of the factual-reality, which may force even more the exclusion of those who do not grasp the knowledge of this new alphabet. There is here a need to generate and manage new ways of thinking so that one is able to guide oneself in this hell of images and labyrinth of information.[3]

Adapting to these New Cultural Changes

In order to tackle the disruptions provoked by this new social situation, some new paths and alternative ways are being conceived. At first some transitional solutions were favored, such as favoring local jobs, voluntary work and the introduction of part-time work.

However, there is also a search for deeper changes – changes that are more in line with conditions such as work-task sharing, signing up to a minimum-wage policy that applies to all people, a redefinition of economic policy and of the democratic system.

The important point here is to make the transition *from a society of full-employment to a society of full-activity*. It has been suggested that this could be achieved through a policy that establishes part-time work for the potentially unemployed, and where they would earn 75 percent of their old wages. For instance, in the case of France, if this policy was implemented and 10 percent of all full-time workers changed to part-time work, it would be able to create 1.5 million new job opportunities.

Another alternative has been suggested by those who do not want productivity to suffer. They have argued that machinery should be kept functioning at 60 hours a week instead of the usual 40 hours. So instead of having one group of full-time workers working 40 hours, there could be two groups of part-time workers working 30 hours. Others have suggested that on top of the part-time wages earned by workers they should also be given a "technological wage." Such a wage would be a kind of social benefit that is given to all part-time workers. This benefit would be funded through a share of a company's profits, profits which are achieved through technological productivity. This share in profits would be transferred to a governmental department which would then pay the "technological wage" to part-time wage earners. Part-time earners would then become used to receiving a benefit, which is independent from their normal wages; this benefit, as mentioned above, is sourced in technological advancements which have both increased productivity and displaced human labor. This benefit would be a kind of compensation for such displacement.

In a globalized economy such a benefit would only be practical if a strong geopolitical group, such as the European Union and the NAFTA (USA, Canada and Mexico), implemented it and maintained it against liberal and competitive market forces.

Thus, there would be a minimum income linked to shared working conditions, which would be guaranteed to all. This income is sometimes called "salary of support" or "salary of citizenship" and it has been strongly defended in Brazil by the senator Eduardo Suplicy of the Partido dos Trabalhadores – PT (Worker's Party). However difficult the implementation of such a benefit, the psychological and social advantages are substantial, as this is a benefit linked to the dignity of life, and as such it is to be added on to already implemented benefits such as free health care, social security benefits, state pension, and free education to all and at all levels, and so on.

Some argue that along with this "salary of support," a "salary of survival" should be granted to the billions of people who live in dire poverty. Moreover, the rich countries, the colonizers, have an ethical obligation to implement such measures. These countries exploited their colonies, which made the accumulation of wealth possible, and this in turn enabled the process of modernization and industrialization. As an imperative of justice, and not of charity, these countries should give a "salary of survival and support" to the dire poor of today's world, who were the colonized of the past. Certainly, such a task would require a re-focusing of the global economy. This would be technically possible if a universal understanding of human dignity became an imperative to all the peoples of the world and if there were a political willingness to implement these benefits.

Full-activity also means that the unemployed should be involved in works that concern the whole of society. For instance, the unemployed could do maintenance work in their cities and towns, their streets, and public buildings. Artists would also be encouraged through an increase in the importance of cultural and spiritual activities that would stimulate dignified co-living in society.

To reconcile the necessity of productivity in societies with the necessity of activity and solidarity among people, it is imperative that economics be redefined. Up until now economics has been the very axis around which the whole of modern society revolves. Development was measured by the economic performance of each society as it sacrificed social and ecological relations. Economic development, or better, material growth, presented itself as an end in itself.

Now it is important to put economics in the service of social development, and economic policy in the service of society and nature's well-being. This is an economy that yields enough and proper production for all, human beings and other sentient beings in nature, and not an economy that yields a material unlimited production which is centered on human beings only. The function of the economy, in its original sense, consists in the management of needs, in the assurance that quantitative vital necessities will be met, in providing access to quality goods and in fulfilling the desires of each individual in solidarity with the desires of others.

Many argue that a new economic paradigm, that is, the multidimensional economy, is necessary if we are to achieve such tasks.[4] A multidimensional economy focuses on fair or just distribution; that is, its focus is on giving to each individual according to his or her necessities, talents and labor. There is a need to qualify the market economy. The predominance of the market economy gives rise to monopolies and cartels, or in other words, the stronger dominates the weaker. In poor countries it is the very origin of the black market economy. Moreover, subscription to this economic trend neither knows nor values other important features of society such as human development, the economy of skills and distribution, and voluntary activities (since these latter do not focus on economic profit but on social benefit). The market economy, when left to its own devices, has a perverse logic: the maximization of yield with the minimal input of capital. However, this logic should apply only to some spheres of the socio-economic process instead of being its central pillar. The market is a central social and democratic entity. It is the very place where supply meets demand and thus where the consuming needs of social agents are taken care of. Hence, we need an economy *with* the market and not an economy *of* market.

The objective of governmental economic policies and of companies that understand the multidimensionality of the economy does not focus on the unlimited production of wealth and of full-employment, but rather on maintaining a stable society of full-activity where there is a sense of co-living, which enables each individual to achieve self-fulfillment.

Economic activity represents a particular human phenomenon and as such it belongs to the biosphere. The eco factor cannot be easily dismissed nowadays and it must be taken into account even more than other criteria in an economic policy that aims at a steady development. Such a policy should aim:

1. To support productive forces and factors, without which deprivation, famine and dire poverty arise.
2. To foment socio-cultural values that accompany changes in the living conditions of societies. Such values are all-encompassing of the whole of society and inhibit cultural unsettling and the sense of a meaningless life.
3. To look after the environment with the use of technology that works with nature and not to the detriment of or against nature. Such technology aims to extract without destroying the environment and to transform without destabilizing the ecosystem.

The role of the state is extremely important if a multidimensional economy is to work. On an historical note, the state has not been a good provider of social services. This is mainly due to the effects of corruption and waste in the provision of these services. The role of the state is, however, indispensable in defining the "rules of the game," safeguarding of the law, ethical processes and in providing the integration of strategic policies that guarantee a steady development that fulfills present demands and that do not damage or hinder future generations.

Just like the state, civil society should also be strengthened. It is in the civil society that a dialogue regarding the welfare of all takes place and that choice regarding the future is defined. It is for this reason that one should not be satisfied with representative democracies only. One should also participate directly in those dialogues and choices so that a more participative democracy emerges. Such a democracy is more environmentally and socially friendly. It is also strengthened by the actions of NGOs (non-governmental organizations) that stimulate civil society into action. Needless to say, NGOs are themselves governed by internal relations of direct and participative democracy.

There is a danger that politicians are not culturally and spiritually equipped to understand the implications of the questions with which they are faced. They make use of solutions and models of past crises and as such they fail to see this great new global revolution that is taking place. Not so much "out with the old and in with the new" as a rehashing of old ideas.

How does this New Society Impinge on the Poor of the World?

Two-thirds of humankind live outside this new society. Their needs are primarily linked to survival and daily tasks. They are in need of established scientific methods and techniques so that the guarantee of a basic hygiene infrastructure with sewage system, drinking water, gas, public transport, schools, proper housing, health centers, security and places for leisure are established in the areas where they live. For them, to modernize means the introduction of the mere essentials for a minimum standard of living conditions. They are, however, a mass that is subordinated to internationally connected national elites that are already part of the new paradigm of society.

These elites introduce the information and communication society and create for themselves small havens where they can directly and selectively take part in this new cultural phase. In the societies of the remaining two-thirds of the world's population, who are poor and marginalized, emerges the spectator-society. This is the society of spectacle and show, a society captivated by TVs, shopping malls, rock music, jazz and sports. Thus, some are able to take part directly in this new cultural phase through modern enclaves where the most modern technology is consumed, while others can only take part through images and the imaginary. The spectator-society accelerates the migration from the countryside and small rural towns to the cities. Migration to the cities occurs because cities are the central stage for the show, the dreams and the imaginary. The shanty-town phenomena that occurred in most countries in the southern hemisphere is a direct consequence of the fascination that the countryside has for the cities. People in the shanty towns may not have food, but they will have a hi-fi system and a TV set. These give them access to the world of images and as such to dreams and desires. The consequence of this is growth in the informal economy as a necessity of survival.

Among the participants of this informal economy there is an emergence of a new kind of solidarity and different sorts of resistance and of struggle. This is, however, occurring with many difficulties because their awareness is so fragmented and formed by residues of so many cultures, such as countryside, urban, modern and informatics cultures. It is impossible to forecast the future of these masses that find themselves marginalized and excluded from this new cultural phase that is based on informatics.

Lastly, it is noteworthy here that the new technologies of informatics and communication will give rise to a new kind of society. Let us now contrast this new emerging society with the current industrial society. Marjorie Jouen and Marc Luyckx schematized the characteristics of both societies rather well, as follows:[5]

Characteristics of the global emerging society

	Current society	Emerging society
Social organization	Passive consumers	Actors or agents capable of expressing themselves culturally/ spectators
	Nanny state	Civil society
	Representative democracy	Participative democracy
	Nations; mercantile societies	Planet Earth/global societies
Relations between government and its people	Hierarchic power	Equal relations
	Distance	Transparency
	Speech	Images
	Information is monopolized by the government	Individuals will re-appropriate themselves of information/ manipulation

Values	Transcendent sense	Immanent sense
	Predominance of the economic	Predominance of the cultural
	Abundance	Prudence
	Adjustment	Co-responsibility
	Freedom	Standard of living and integration

Methodological Issues

What should we do in order to gain consistency in the profile of this new emerging society? Below are some insights that are the outcome of recent studies on this issue.

Rethink Human Relations with the Truth

One must pay attention to the methodological matter if one wishes to face the current cultural changes in a liberated and unbiased manner. An instance of this is the fact that the new information technologies have shifted the conception of truth as well as how truth is achieved.

Our cultural tradition developed two approaches to truth. The first approach is an epistemological take that understands truth is the conformity of the representations in our mind with reality. The second approach is an ontological take that understands truth is whatever is revealed to us by reality itself. The experience of truth in one's life is called truthfulness. That is to say, one must be a good listener and an attentive spectator of whatever is revealed. Also, truth was usually propagated through spoken words and written texts.

The emerging society, the information society, works with the use of images and scenarios. It increasingly tries to capture reality's movements and configurations through its complex relations and contexts. Human beings take part in these scenarios. They seize truth as they set about adapting themselves to the changing scenarios. Truth means to capture the sense of the scenario, relative to the totality of reality, and which is itself (reality) characterized by complexity, contradiction, supplementation and evolution. Order-disorder-order constitute the underlying force of reality as maintained by Ilya Prigogine. To get bogged down by the text and by the truth that is said and revealed in the same text is to fix oneself to a particular moment in the scenario of history and as such it is to lose the open and evolving meaning of this truth.

The information society has great difficulties dealing with the authoritative (top to bottom), totalitarian and fundamentalist manner of truth communication (i.e. the assumption that "outside our views there is no truth"). The new technologies of information enable individuals to re-appropriate power and images/words. These individuals are neither architects nor the deliverers of top to bottom messages; rather they are co-producers and co-authors of information. The very nature of information is communicability, and, as such, it is also democratic.

Towards a Dialectic Reasoning and a Holistic Philosophy of Life

Our culture is underlined by a linear form of reasoning and by a unidirectional kind of causality – thus, the reason for the influence of the law of identity and of the law of the excluded middle. The main focus of the new understanding of reality, however, rests on becoming aware of the complex features of reality – this is dialectical reasoning. To know is linked to not-knowing; opposites and antonyms are not negations of reality, but manifestations of its plurality; chaos and order are utterly linked. Human beings, themselves, are simultaneously *sapiens* and *demens*, that is to say, human beings are rational beings but also they are beings of excesses and dementia. In the light of this, it is important to go beyond the kind of discourse that romantically imagines that the people know best and, as such, is able to envisage better perspectives for the future. It is also important to go beyond the arrogance of academics, technocrats and politicians who do not see the limits of their own knowledge and ignorance. Ignorance is one who imagines other people to be ignorant.

The view that reality has many complex features avoids extreme, black and white answers, and thus it is especially useful in trying to resolve conflicts. For instance, in international negotiations one can frequently see the confrontation between those who do not like protectionism and who try to push forward new sorts of agreements, and those who want to maintain the privileges gained by rich countries (to the detriment of the rest of the world) and who stall any talk on this subject. The solution to this problem lies with the so-called win–win law of John Nash, which requires the introduction of new agents in these negotiations, such as representatives of the world civil society, unions, religious leaders, ecologists, indigenous communities, and so on. The conflict in international negotiations shows clearly that there is an economic war between rich countries, who also form a "league" against poorer ones. This fact calls for an economic armistice between rich and poor nations; or, better said, it calls for an "economic disarmament" of rich countries (note: "economic disarmament" is a term coined by Ricardo Petrella who is a former coordinator of the sciences and technology projects of the European Union). At the same time it would be sensible to adopt policies such as the taxation of any produce that harms the environment; invest in the development of technologies that are appropriate to the various ecological regions of the world; and to face up to the collective problems that threaten a great number of human beings, such as famine, diseases, homelessness, unemployment, and so on. Hence, only a dialectical and inclusive form of reasoning is appropriate to the complexities of our current reality.

Recover Subdued Initiatives from the Memory of Cultures

Each culture has in its own memory a great deal of initiatives that did not have the chance of being implemented, or that, for various reasons, failed. And so, for instance, being paid a salary is a relatively new development. In the past a particular notion of labor predominated, a notion that linked remuneration to criteria such as need, social class, worked hours, creativity, talents, and so on. Nowadays, with the rise of the society of activity along with the society of waged labor one finds the need to bring back a modality of remuneration other than salary. The American Indians and African tribes are community-based cultures. These cultures always produced collectively and always in a sustainable and ecological manner. They do not understand labor as a meaningless exploration of natural resources; rather they understand labor as supporting the Earth-mother in the production of goods that are necessary to life in general and to the commonwealth of all. Colonization and the current mentality centered on production have undermined these other approaches to labor and remuneration. Today, however, these alternatives can be a model to be followed in the pursuit of productive processes that do not harm nature, as well as helping the re-awakening of original populations and cultures.

The Necessity of Order and Hierarchy in Images

The production of images is currently anarchic and the abundance of messages is unlimited. Such a situation could lead to possible manipulation, tricking and falsification which could be used for political reasons and in mass communication. The limits of truth and falsity are blurred and the level of truth in representations as well as the credibility of such representations are increasingly more difficult to verify.

The image has created a new form of writing and a new alphabet. These are not merely created; rather, they are carefully planned and aimed at producing an outcome. Thus, these must be read and interpreted carefully within a context just as we have done with the common writings and alphabet.

We can sink ourselves into virtual images and navigate virtual realities. The symbolic and imaginary record of these images and realities is the same as in the actual reality. The subject participating in such simulations may have her behavior altered. It is possible to create a set of images with sexual, sadistic, masochistic and brutal natures. Chat-rooms on the

Internet, especially, have changed human intercourse, even in close relations. On the one hand these represent a new form of virtual communion between human beings where everything is *on line*; on the other hand there is the possibility of pretence, conning, lies and falsifications that can even lead to crimes.

It is necessary for human beings to adopt an ethical attitude, to perceive various points of view, to understand and communicate a message and its degree of humanistic veracity or of ideological falsity, and to be aware of underlying meanings. These issues are directly connected to other more basic matters such as: What is a human being? What is his or her vocation? What are the necessary conditions for him or her to continue to be a human being? What are the necessary conditions for human beings to co-live with the totality of nature (human beings as part of nature and not as an entity over and above nature)?

The human psyche and the capacity that human beings have to guide themselves are confused by the world of virtual images and by the vast amount of information and products offered by it. Comblin rightly noted that what is seen is just as important as what is not seen, what is known is as important as what is not known and what is informed just as important as what is not informed. To learn could be as important as not to learn. The amount of images on offer could lead to a loss of connection with the actual reality. Human beings cannot live in a virtual world of representations and inhabit images even if these seem more real than the actual reality. Perhaps the excess of "reality" of the virtual world gives it away as an artificial and fake realm; this is so because the actual world is opaque, contradictory, holistic, sapiens and demens, concrete and potential. Human beings require direct and immediate contact with the complexities, contradictions, obscurities, luminosities and challenges of the actual reality. They need to fulfill the vocation ascribed to them by evolution, that is, they need to become co-creators and co-pilots of nature. The human being needs to be always with and not against nature, exactly because he or she is both part of nature as a whole and an ethical being who takes responsibility for what happens to the world.

2 The Process of Globalization

The *second* body of data revealing support for the view that a global civilization has arisen is the accelerated process of globalization. This process is not new, however. Its historical roots go back to the sixteenth century, more precisely to the year 1521, when Magellan, for the first time, circumnavigated the world, and thus empirically proved that the Earth was round. From this, the path to the westernization of the planet was open. Europe started the colonialist and imperialist adventure which conquered all lands, and which put these to the service of European interests. These interests encompassed the search for power and riches, the imposition of white western culture, the forced implementation of Christianity, and the fierce defense of individualism. It is noteworthy here to mention that from the perspective of victims of this process, victims who are based in the southern hemisphere, this adventure was conducted by all sorts of violent methods, genocide, ethnocide (i.e. death of particular populations) and ecocide (i.e. death of ecosystems). This is the 'Age of Iron' of human history, in the well-coined expression by Edgar Morin.[1] No matter how many contradictions this age has, it is from it that the bases for the process of globalization were launched, a process greatly accelerated today.

The process of globalization is occurring on different fronts. Let us assess some of these.

Globalization through the Economy and Single Markets

The more visible process of globalization can be seen in the increasing interdependence of countries' economies and through the integration of markets, forming a single market. It is important to point out here that this interdependence of countries' economies is, in fact, a dependence of peripheral countries on core countries, because the relations between countries are neither equal nor symmetrical, and without such relations there is no real interdependence. In fact, there is a profound technological, financial, political, and ideological dependence from countries which have not managed to develop themselves in a continuous and stable manner to countries who have. However, it is also a fact that no country nowadays is self-sufficient and has the solution for its problems within its own borders. For instance, the solution for Germany's or for Brazil's problems are not to be found exclusively within Germany and Brazil, but in the kind of rapport that these countries establish with other countries. What occurs in one country will impinge on the whole of the world.

Thus, for example, one may ask: why did the large plantations of coca plant (which is the raw material for cocaine production) appear in Colombia? It appeared due to the international crises in the commodities market of coffee beans. Instead of coffee, the peasant farmers started to plant the coca plant. Coca planting creates a market. From this market emerge the drug cartels. The drug cartels generate a great deal of cash. This cash needs to be laundered before it can enter the legal financial markets. It is laundered in the tax havens of the Bahamas or in the Swiss banks, which, like the other international banks, fail to distinguish between money that is sourced in proper production and money which is sourced in drugs, international arms commerce and corruption. Everything is money, *pecunia non olet*, the Romans used to say ("money does not smell"). After being laundered, this capital returns to the market or it is used to finance other illicit activities, such as gambling, internationally organized prostitution, or the buying and selling of arms which are sent to war zones wherever these may be in the world.

Another example of this interdependence is the following. Let us take Germany. In order for Germany to finance the process of reunification with the former DDR, the German government decided to increase its interest rates. Higher interest rates attract foreign investment, particularly from neighboring countries, such as France and Britain. These countries, to avoid the bleeding of its financial markets, also increased their interest rates, and thus also attracted foreign investment. Poor countries which are in constant need of financial loans to support their development find themselves obliged to pay higher interest rates, and hence increase their national debt. The high interest rates also impinge on their importing capabilities, so that the technological gap between the peripheral countries and core countries is widened.

It thus becomes clear that economies are intertwined. On the one hand, there is a bigger union between markets and nations; on the other hand, however, there is a bigger division due to the dependence of the weak on the strong. This situation creates just as much equality as it creates inequality, both in world proportions. It is due to this situation that 17 percent of the world's population consume 80 percent of all produce, and only 20 percent of all production must satisfy all the necessities of 73 percent of humankind. Is there any logic, any human sense, any benevolence, in such data?

Adding to this is the fact that the control of information, of accumulated technological and scientific knowledge, and the capacity to innovate, constitute the most valuable commodities in the international market. These are the most well-guarded reserve of core countries in this internationally integrated system. It is from these oligopolies that the relation of dependence is kept within the more general regime of interdependence.

Three factors, according to M. Arruda and R. A. Dreifuss, drive the process of globalization on the economic front:

1.   The first is the rise of mega conglomerates and strategic corporations, which act at a global level and in various sectors of the economy. These are not the old-fashioned multinationals, but global companies, since they operate having the whole of the world and its markets in mind, and not merely various nations and regional markets (an example of such is the Mitsubishi conglomerate). Its Japanese operational base operates in some 90 different sectors. Something similar is true of the ASEA-Brown Bovery in the heavy manufacturing sector, or the Daimler-Benz in the arms and automobiles sector, or the Novartis-Ciba-Geigy in the pharmaceutical, chemical and agro-industrial sectors. These conglomerates make alliances among themselves, alliances which are not based on their national subscription. These inter-conglomerate alliances create a web of very complex global relations, with very few concerns for their own original nation or people, and which allows them to avoid being subjected to any sort of scrutiny of their global activities. An example of this is the partnership between the Ford group (USA) and the Mazda group (Japan) which compete against the trans-cultural alliances of Chrysler-Mitsubishi, Chrysler-Maserati, General Motors-Isuzu, Fiat-Nissan, and Globo of Brazil with Time-Life. All these conglomerates act at a global level with great flexibility, securing markets and lucrative advantages.

2.   There is also a continental focus within the wider process of globalization, such as the Japanese bloc and the Asian Tiger economies, the NAFTA (USA, Mexico, and Canada), the European Union, and the Mercosul (Brazil, Argentina, Uruguay, and Paraguay). Among the first three above-mentioned blocs, there exists true economic wars as each bloc tries to gain more and more hegemony at the international level. This causes enormous technological progress, but at the same time it worsens the ecological crisis, and it either marginalizes or totally excludes developing countries.

3.   There is also the rise of trans-national elites which aim at the political and economic management of the Earth, and which also undermines the role of the state and of national elites. The state needs to be redefined so that it can adapt itself to these world changes, since these changes occur beyond the limits of nation-states. Not even the consequences of the awful ecological degradation respects the political limits of nations. The responsibility for these is collective and transcends nation-states.

Hence, the issue of the process of globalization through economic processes brings with it an important issue, which requires an urgent solution: How does one create minimal social satisfaction at the personal, community, national, continental, and global level, which keeps humankind united and without reasons to wage wars for the survival of the two-thirds who live in poverty in the great South? Two-thirds of the world's population up until now have been marginalized and excluded from technological benefits. They do not accept peacefully the death sentence that hangs over their heads. There is a great risk that humankind will split itself into two: on one side, there is a small number that has access to biotechnological advances and "full health," and who achieve the life expectancy of the "cells," 120 or 130 years; and, on the other side, is the majority of humankind surviving in the current ways and who have a life expectancy of 60 or 70 years old.

The issue of a minimal social satisfaction re-introduces a question about socialism. Socialism presents itself as a political form more adequate (than others) to tackle the global social demands, even those demands that are concerned with nature. Without the socialization of ways of life and of the scarce natural resources of the Earth, there is no certain way to guarantee either the survival of the majority of human beings or the biosphere, of which human beings are part and parcel. Again, one must advocate for a social democracy, which is ecologic, global and cosmic, just as has been postulated earlier.

Globalization through Ideals, Spirituality, and Wars

The process of globalization occurs primarily under the economic banner. But together with economics comes other factors, such as ideologies, the spiritual quest, values and even wars. It is a fact that from the West many ideas and values emerged which nowadays enter into the world consciousness and are part of the syllabus of any school. Christianity, in its various versions, had an extremely important function in spreading these ideas and values. Christianity spread wherever it went, usually as an imperialist tool, the sense of human dignity and its eternal destination, and moreover, of its transcendence from the powers of this world. It always announced the importance of love, of solidarity, and of benevolence for the establishment of social relations, which are fair in this world and fortuitous in the afterlife.

For instance, the Enlightenment captured the world with its idealist vision of human beings as rational beings, and because of this, as a being with the capacity of being mature and autonomous, a being with the capacity of deciding the path to be followed, and a being able to submit all traditional institutions which controlled traditions and ideas to his or her critical judgment. It is thanks to this movement that schools have been implemented throughout the world.

The French revolution awoke in the world the idea of citizen's rights and made of equality, liberty, and fraternity the most efficacious revolutionary banners up to that moment in history.

Evolutionism showed that all beings have a common denominator. Everything has a genesis. This leads to the rise of the concept of time, and of scientific irreversibility. It was a great achievement of Darwin to show the unity of the human species from a common primate. It was left to Teillard de Chardin to elaborate a perspective of global understanding which included in the process of evolution the Christian phenomena. The cosmogenesis supports the biogenesis that supports the anthropogenesis that supports the christogenesis, which is grounded in the teogenesis. In this way, human beings and God are integrated in the universe. The problem of living and non-living entities is also overcome, since both classical science, and the more modern science of Einstein, understand that life – the most extraordinary phenomena of reality – was placed at the margins of scientific investigations, especially with respect to investigations in physics; life was left to the domains of miracles, religions, and in the best scenario, such as advocated by J. Monod, to a fluke that remains constant; life was not related to matter; under the evolutionary perspective of a structured universe, however, life has its origins in a less miraculous way. Like Prigogine demonstrated so well, and before him Boltzmann, life roots itself in the properties of matter, when it is put in unbalanced settings, or chaotic and unordered situations. What happens in such situations is that chaos becomes creative and unordered situations the start of a new order. The second principle of thermodynamics, that everything evolves towards a complete lack of heat (i.e. entropy), has a new sense here. Thermodynamically human beings are evolving "top down" towards their death, but at the same time, human beings are evolving "bottom up" towards more and more complex forms of life thanks to the dissipative structures of entropy. Life is within the potentialities of the universe's matter that reveals itself as the true mother (just as the etymology of the word suggest, *mater* = mother = matter). Matter is the mother of all things, of mass, of energy, of information-communication, of life. Matter is also spiritual, smooth, mysterious, and deserving of much fascination and contemplation by mystics, such as the psalmists, Saint Francis or Teillard de Chardin, within our cultural tradition.

Modern cosmology enabled us to comprehend that the universe is a homogenous process that is unique, complex, contradictory and complementary, and which unites all beings, living and non-living, through a web of relations in such a way that nothing can exist without these very relations. This cosmology offers us a scientific cornerstone which is indispensable if one is to think about globalization as a moment of an infinitely bigger process where there is a convergence of energies, beings, minds, and hearts – a process which has always been in place in the universe, and which has a mysterious meaning that may only be understood from a transcendent and religious perspective.

Another factor in globalization consists in the hunger and thirst for spirituality, in the meditation about the meaning of life, and about the crucial meaning of this technological adventure which human beings have undertaken for the past 400 years. The conviction grows that it is not enough to both accumulate and have more, and know more about the universe and expand our horizons; it is also important to develop one's capacity to experience, dialogue and learn through intercourse with the other, and through contact with the Absolute, which is conventionally called God.

When I refer to spirituality here, what is meant by this concept is more within its anthropologic meaning and less within its more specific religious sense. Spirituality means the capacity that human beings, men and women, have of connecting with their most inner and deep thoughts, and enter into a state of harmony through the pleas that come from their interior. Those who consider themselves as part of a religious denomination, together with agnostics and non-believers, can do this connecting. Each individual encounters their own structure of desire, their own horizon of utopia, with the masculine and feminine inside themselves, with the universe of their inner self. The process of personalization presupposes the integration of all these dimensions which confer importance, serenity, and peace to human life. Certainly, for the religious person this process is inhered in God, and to dialogue and embrace this process implicates both embracing the unconditional love of God and listening for His word. It is very evident nowadays, in all parts of the world, from the West to the East, that people are searching for spiritual ways of meditating both about the divine which inhere in us and about interiorization.

This spirituality engages with modern cosmology, that is to say, with the new image of the world that emerges from the sciences, from the so-called "deep" psychology of Jung *et al.*, from transpersonal psychology, from the changes in theoretical physics, from the works of Einstein, Heisenberg, Bohr, Hawking, and especially Prigogine and Stengers (with its dissipative structures, where life consumes energy from its environment and tries to escape entropy), and from the much discussed and criticized new paradigm of Capra.

If pre-modern cosmology was static, unitarian, hierarchical, authoritarian, and sacred, symbolized by the staircase that united heaven to Earth; if the modern vision of the world (as from Galileo and Newton) is dualist (matter and spirit), rational, instrumental, scientific and secular, represented by the image of the machine; then contemporary cosmology, in the current phase of cultural mutation (I prefer to use contemporary to "post-modern"), is fundamentally holistic, non-hierarchical, participative and spiritual, symbolized by the metaphor of a game-play or dance. Together with spirit and matter, life enters into consideration with its non-linear logic, with its complexities, its organization, and its auto-regulations. The synthetic perspective, which is holistic, is more important than the analytic perspective. According to the synthetic perspective the human being is not a passive spectator of the world's show, but an active actor, who is always included in the sciences and research, no matter how objective these are. The metaphor of the game-play explains the non-linear logic well. A non-linear form of reasoning embraces the complexities of reality, and it requires the participation of the game-players, and it must also cater for their creativity. Human beings search for self-understanding as a fundamental dialectical unity; that is, they search the integration of their intelligence, feelings and inner selves and they try to integrate themselves within the wider bio-network. God emerges, not from outside of the totality, but from within as the substance which unites everything or as the common denominator that supports everything. There is a lack of terminology to account for this emergent trend. Explaining this further, everything is in God and God is in everything. This is the so-called panentheism (God in everything and everything in God), which differs from pantheism (where everything, no matter how different, is God). A whole range of accounts coming from various cultures is witnessing this new trend.

The process of globalization occurs also through history, especially in moments of dissolution and wars. In three great conflicts virtually all of the Earth was involved. In the First World War (1914–1918), in the Second World War (1939–1945) and in the Gulf War (1991). In the air, in the sea, on land and on all fronts nations and armies confronted one another. One hundred million people found themselves involved in the Second World War. Fifteen million soldiers and another thirty-five million civilians died. The Gulf War against Iraq forced virtually all countries in the world to take a stance. During that war, humanity showed a sinister solidarity in its desire to destroy and kill; the images transmitted directly from the battlegrounds exemplified, in real time, the Earth's union in shame, since it was a battle between the mighty Goliath against the little David. The same cowardly logic prevailed during the Second Gulf War unleashed by President George Bush of the USA, contrary to the will of the UN and the majority of humankind, against Saddam Hussein's Iraq in 2003.

After the First World War the first organization to express the rise of this new global reality was created, the League of Nations. At the end of the Second World War a new organization was projected, an organization that hosted representatives of all governments on Earth, the UN, which embodies globalization as a political event.

During the past few years two issues have revealed the advanced level of globalization: the danger of weapons of mass destruction, such as chemical, biological and nuclear weapons, and the problematic state of ecology. For the first time in the history of humankind, human beings have invented ways of destruction and death which can destroy humankind many times, and threaten the biosphere. These are the nuclear and chemical weapons devised by the superpowers, such as the USA and the USSR. The alert of a threat to the biosphere was first sounded in 1972 by the Club of Rome, where there was an acknowledgment, in a nutshell, that the kind of technological and industrial developments in both the Western and Communist countries imply a systematic aggression against Nature, a slow consumption of non-renewable resources, and the downgrading of the quality of life of human beings and other beings. Moreover, the dramatic scarcity of fresh water (only 0.7 percent of all water is fit for human consumption), the greenhouse effect, and the hole in the ozone layer can produce dreadful effects in the biosphere. Death shows its face through the mask of biocide (death of life), ecocide (death of ecosystems), and geocide (death of the Earth).

Globalization through Politics

The West has been trying to globalize itself for at least two centuries. Liberalism, with its supremacy of capital and ideological expressions, imposed itself throughout the world in a slow but steady manner as socio-political modes of organization that are very similar to each other. Practically all peoples turned themselves into nation-states. Democracy has penetrated the political habits of all traditions, be it as a universal value to be lived in all levels of human intercourse (family, school, institutions), be it as the form to organize the society and the state's power. Thus, under international pressure, liberal democracies have risen and continue to rise; these are liberal democracies that are representative of the people, and in certain cases, of a popular and social nature.

With the democratic forms of relations and exercise of power, also grows the awareness of human rights – individual, social, and ecological rights of the minorities and peoples. Democracy only functions when, previous to its implementation, an atmosphere favorable to the respect and promotion of societies and individuals' rights was instilled. With democracy also comes the ethical view that human beings are ends in themselves and never a means, and that all power is only legitimized if balanced under the mediation of justice, the commonwealth of all citizens and nature, and when all technological development is focused on the promotion of integration of the human being itself, and the various peoples.

Another factor in the implementation of the process of globalization is represented by the same kind of rapport with nature that all countries are assuming. This is done through scientific and technological projects. Through these projects human beings have deeply modified the face of Earth, by introducing a second-hand kind of nature, creating thinking and acting habits that are, today, trans-cultural and which are making human experience more homogeneous.

There are increasingly strong signs that we need to devise a new global political order, a new order with centers and organs of power that serve the global questions, and which are open to a world government. The UN, the Security Council, the IMF, the World Bank, and other organizations lead us in this direction. However, they are dominated by the controlling mechanisms and decision-making processes that are either the outcome of the Second World War, or dominated by the G8, and which follow a political paradigm based in blocs that dominate world politics. The overlap of all major problems faced by nations is because of the inter-global-dependence point towards the formulation of global solutions, especially to those problems concerned with the ecological price of development, and of the production of food and minimal infrastructure for those two-thirds of the world's people who are poor and marginalized.

3   The Rise of a New Global Consciousness

The decisive factor that reveals the rise of a new civilization is, surely, the new level of consciousness that is increasingly taking root in society – this is the global consciousness. Teilhard de Chardin had already maintained in 1933 that: "The age of Nation states is gone. If we do not want to perish it is time for us to leave our prejudices behind us and shape the Earth. Earth will only become conscious of itself through the predicament of changes and transformations."

This predicament has deeply established itself in people's minds: we are co-responsible for our common destiny (both human and Earth's destiny) since we constitute a cohesive unity of multiplicities.

On April 12, 1961 Yuri Gagarin orbited the Earth for the first time. Since that day a new perspective has entered human consciousness: we started to see the Earth from outside. The image of Neil A. Armstrong and Edwin Aldrin landing on the surface of the moon with Apollo 11 on July 21, 1969 had an even bigger impact.

The simple words of John W. Young, one of the American astronauts who participated in the fifth trip to the moon on April 16, 1972, revealed this new consciousness: "Down there is the Earth, this white and blue planet, extremely beautiful, awesome, our human fatherland. From the Moon I am able to hold it in my hand. And from this perspective there are no white or black, nor East and West, nor Communists and Capitalists, nor North and South. Earth encompasses us all. We need to learn to love this planet since we are part and parcel of it." From that day he promised himself that, on his return home, he would dedicate himself entirely to the pedagogy of love of the planet Earth.

It is a fact, that when the Earth is seen from the outside, the understanding that it is part of a larger system arises, an understanding that the Earth is part of the solar system, of the galaxy, and of the expanding universe. The Earth's sun is a star among a hundred billion stars in the Milky Way, which in turn, is a constellation among billions of larger constellations. We are 27,000 light years from the center of our galaxy, a galaxy that appeared eight billion years after the big bang; we are in a medium-sized solar system that appeared eleven billion years after the dawn of the universe; we live on a miniscule planet, Earth, that has existed for four and a half billion years.

Earth, however, when seen from the outside, materializes itself as an organic totality. We do not live on Earth. We are Earth (*adamah-adam, humus-homo-human*) and part of the Earth.[1] There is a web of inter-relations between human societies, the biosphere, the surface of our planet, the mountains, the oceans, the atmosphere and life and potential life. These are not merely parts of a whole; rather they are part of an organic whole. Everything is interdependent forming a unique and complex system. If life and matter were to oppose themselves, then we would have, on the one side, the *mechanical-material world*, and on the other side the *biological world* (and within this the *human world*) set apart from each other and necessitating God to act as the bridge between these different realms. In truth, we could do without such an idea. Matter cannot be seen as something static anymore, but as something that has active, creative and informative characteristics. The universe's dynamics is the common ground that underlies, unifies and diversifies all levels of being.

Such views enabled the formulation of the Gaia thesis by the British scientist John E. Lovelock. According to this thesis, Gaia (i.e. the mythological Greek name for the Earth) is a supra-organism that maintains the right balance of physical, chemical and energetic elements through its dynamic powers in such a way that life and evolution are enabled and supported. Just as cells are part of organs and organs part of a body, in a similar manner beings are part of an ecosystem, which is part of the Earth-system, which is part of the cosmos-system. All elements act and interact in a synchronized manner so that the dynamics of the system is maintained (through chaos and order) and thus enabling and supporting life.

The level of oxygen in the atmosphere is 21 percent; the level of salt in the oceans has been, for billions of years, 3.4 percent – a level that is maintained through the dynamic action of bacteria, micro-organisms in the depths of the seas and in the Earth's crust; the Earth's crust also has an average constant temperature of between 15 and 35 degrees. Should the level of oxygen rise to 25 percent then when lightning struck formidable fires would destroy large parts of the Earth's forests. If the level of salt rose to 6 percent, it would make impossible much marine life. And, if the temperature of the Earth rose by 5 or 7 degrees, it would make existence impossible for the majority of terrestrial life.

Life came out of the Earth and its development enabled human life. If the supra-organism Earth generates intelligent beings such as human beings, then I maintain that this is clear evidence that the Earth itself functions following intelligent principles of higher levels and with a cumulated memory of billions of years. Amazingly, a single cell of skin contains all of the information about human life; somewhat like a library, any cell contains the biological memory of the universe. This is a strong argument for maintaining that Earth-Gaia is alive and generating life.

All beings have a similar genetic code. The differences found between a amoeba, a dinosaur, a hummingbird and a human being is due to different combinations of the same genetic alphabet. The genetic alphabet cannot exist without the chemical and physical elements that are inherent to it.

Thus everything is encompassed by the life-system. It is neither rhetoric nor romanticism to call, like Saint Francis did, all beings brothers and sisters. There is a physical and chemical basis to the relationship between beings. In fact, we are all cosmic brothers and sisters.

The species *homo* has increasingly discovered its humanity through the diverse and complex unity of human beings with their cultures, histories, institutions and share of the biosphere, which in turn is connected by the planet Earth. These human beings are simultaneously *sapiens* and *demens*. That is to say, they are rational, creative, and purposeful beings (*sapiens*). And, at the same time, they create absurdities, utter violence and destruction (*demens*). On the one hand, we have the globalization of various cultural traditions that link themselves in a productive manner. On the other hand, there is a certain rejection of this globalization by entire regions of the globe, such as in the former Yugoslavia and various former republics of the USSR, where there is an opposition to certain religions, cultural habits and ethnic groups. Both positions are part of the same contradictory and complementary global process towards an unstoppable globalization.

Until recently the unity of the human species was based on a bio-socio-anthropologic categorization. There was an emphasis on historical and cultural differences as well as on knowledge and technological achievements. Nowadays, however, a new kind of unity has emerged due to the process of globalization. This unity is woven together by collective elements, such as the same approach to nature; similar social organizations; the same reverence towards the human condition; certain kinds of images that are expressed in films and magazines that are released globally; certain kinds of music such as rock and jazz; the organization of labor and leisure; the standardization of certain devices which are accessible to large parts of humanity such as white goods, TV sets, hi-fis, cars and bicycles; the way in which professionals are trained and the manner that their common language is established; and by a collective feeling of responsibility for the future of the planet Earth.

Moreover, we are experiencing today what H. Gadamer called years ago the fusion of horizons or *Horizontverzchmelzung*. Different religious traditions and perspectives of the world are meeting each other. Instead of emphasizing the differences there is a tendency today of underlining the similarities. The teachings of Sufis, Taoists, Zen Buddhists, the Upanishads and the Bhagavad Gita are not merely ancient lessons of enlightenment about mysticism and the divine that come from the Middle and Far East. They are lessons about humanity. Because these are primarily human lessons, they can be understood and enter into dialogue with other traditions. And, as such, they slowly constitute a new meaningful perspective of creative and enriching syncretism. This new perspective is neither Western nor Eastern; it is simply human and global.

This new global consciousness turns us into global citizens, so that we are no longer citizens of this or that country. We live a common destiny. The destiny of the human species is interconnected with the destiny of the planet and of the cosmos. Anthropocentrism is out of place. In fact, we are cosmos- and-Earth-centered. We must place ourselves in the wider system of life and not just on the grouping of peoples, races and nations. We are creatures of the Earth, expressions of the conscious part of this planet, and as such we must democratically co-live with other beings and share justly the means to subsist with them.

All these elements give rise, slowly, to a cosmopolitan and global culture, which is something that has never been seen before in the history of human-kind. Such an event is important not just for the *homo* species but for the whole of the planetary and cosmological processes.

The new consciousness leads us to ask distressing questions: What is our place in the planetary and cosmic processes? What is our mission as conscious beings that are expressions of the consciousness of the cosmos? This new consciousness is a new challenge faced by contemporary anthropology and theology.

4 The Direction of the Current Globalization Process: Is this the Creation of a Noosphere?

Ilya Prigogine, winner of the Nobel Prize for Chemistry in 1977, and his followers, have showed that the passage of time and evolution follow a pattern that increasingly creates complex auto-organized, diverse and inter-retro-related entities. Evolution is not linear; rather, it jumps. An instance of this is the formation of the brain in embryos. After eight weeks of gestation there is a frenetic production of nervous cells, namely, the neurons, in the embryo – and we still do not know the reasons why this happens. Millions of these neurons are produced everyday. After 35 days, however, this process slows down and a new process initiates, the inter-connection of all these neurons, which are the basis for the mental capacity. Other instances that evolution follows such a pattern can be seen all around us. Moreover, the inter-connections between entities do not stop with the neurons; they also occur within the family, the community, society and the planet. There emerges a pan-connection that is very characteristic of the age we live in.

Teilhard de Chardin had an insight about evolution: the more evolution progresses the more complex it becomes; the more complex the more internalized; the more internalized the more self-conscious it becomes; the more self-conscious the more self-creating it becomes, forming a unity over and above its parts.

Are we not today creating the conditions for a higher level of humanization with the increasing complexity of the means of communication, the growing interdependence between entities, the feeling of unification that humanity is experiencing and the accelerated process of globalization? Are we not creating today the conditions for a global and complex web of inter-linked minds?

The jumps in evolution can occur at any moment; it only requires enough accumulated energy to do so. The vast number of human brains currently at work along with the accumulation of knowledge and experiences, the increasing understanding of globalization, the perception that we are co-responsible for what may happen to nature and to humankind enable us to put forward Teilhard's thesis of noosphere, that is, a collective consciousness or the unification of human minds. We are at the dawn of an event that has never been seen before in the history of our planet. That is to say, that one of the elements of our planet, human beings, is on the verge of forming an organic unity. This unification will not occur just through knowledge, but also especially through love. Love is the highest form of unification between all human beings with all human beings, and between all human beings with everything else.

Globalization with all its contradictions and with the victimization of so many people and so many beings of nature causes its dialectical opposite. There is some evidence that there exists the possibility of extra-sensorial communication between minds, or ESP; the phenomena of synchronicity. Rupert Sheldrake's thesis of biological morphogenetic fields maintains that over and above the genetic code that provides the chemical compounds that enable life, there is also the invisible field that cannot be reached by any of the senses, which explains how the elements of the genetic code link themselves together in specific forms and structures, or better said, in systems. This is similar to the gravitational and magnetic fields, which are spatial, invisible structures that can only be verified by their effects. For instance, when iron filings are put around a magnet they reveal its magnetic field. Something similar occurs with life. It is not enough for TV sets to be switched on. The TV set does not produce images. Images are relayed from a source. Similarly, the theory of the morphogenetic field maintains that when an experience, an act, is successful it will resonate over all inter-related beings. Such resonance avoids the loss of this new experience and after it has been repeated and reproduced a number of times all members of the same system will incorporate it. The new experience starts to be reproduced over and over and it helps guarantee the development of life. Hence, within humankind there is currently a significant accumulation of resonance that is leading us towards a global unity. When this accumulation of resonance reaches a critical point it will cause the global unity to emerge as an historical fact.

Historical processes are on the increase. Between 15,000 and 8000 BC there was the Neolithic agricultural revolution. It is fair to say that virtually all cultures have incorporated this revolution. The Industrial Revolution only occurred 30 centuries afterwards, between 1750 and 1850 AD. Relatively soon after this event, one century after, there was the nuclear revolution. Ten years later the information revolution occurred with the decoding of the genetic code. The spiral of evolution unfolds itself in an increasingly rapid manner. Some even expect that the start of this new millennium will witness a new beginning; this new beginning would be marked by the rise of a noosphere, a collective consciousness. Such a fact would mark a new *katun*, that is, a new global age for Earth, in the language of the Mayas, who speculated a great deal about such events. Thus, a new phase for humanity would be established, a new phase where humanity would be united, diverse and convergent.

Humanity, due to its cooperative talents and abilities, would function as a sort of brain of the planet Earth. The more human beings understand and act in a synchronized manner with the Earth, the more they would promote the development of nature – and the less they would act against nature. The more human beings discover and understand the hidden capacities of Earth the more creative beings they will become, being able even to interfere in the process of evolution by accelerating it or slowing it down. Humanity would become Earth insofar as Earth thinks, desires, characterizes, plans, dreams and loves.

Everything that each human being does or does not do impinges on the creation of this new phase of humanity. Hence, it is important for each individual to connect with the Earth and with its destiny; it is important that everything that is done by us should be done with a proper understanding and having in mind all that is around us and the cosmos itself. We are helping Gaia to move forward and fully achieve her purpose, a purpose that includes us, life itself, self-consciousness, the connection between the Spirit and matter, the synchronization between everything with everything in the face of the mystery of God.

5 Christianity's Contribution to the New Civilization

The emerging phenomenon of this new civilization represents a challenge to all religions and to Christianity in particular. Before proceeding it must be acknowledged that this new reality brings with it a new understanding of the Mystery of the world. This Mystery emerges with a feeling of awe about the universe's grandiosity and complexity. This feeling of awe is connected to a new experiencing of Being, of the Sacred and a new encounter with the Spirit of the world or *Weltgeist*.

There are some in this emerging civilization, especially those connected to the physical sciences (such as ecology, biology, astronautics, quantum physics, and so on) that show some new age or mystical inclinations (and this is linked to the word Mystery). I do not wish to take up this issue here since I have dealt with it in another book of mine.[1]

I want to raise here two questions for Christianity. First, I want to enquire to what extent this new civilization forces Christianity to re-think itself, and in doing so, to go back to its original ideals. Secondly, I wish to investigate to what extent this self-criticized and revitalized Christianity helps the global civilization to express itself religiously and to revere the Sacred that is manifested in itself also.

Only a Christianity that is One of Liberation and Willing to Exchange Ideas can be Globalized

Despite the fact that the process of globalization has started in the West it cannot signify the supremacy of Western, White and Christian culture. The new civilization encompasses and transforms elements of all cultures and of the great religious traditions within the context of a global consciousness, of a new kind of citizenship, namely, a global citizenship, and of a new alliance with nature.

This very premise questions the way Christianity has presented itself. With very few exceptions, in its various denominations Christianity was a religion of conquest and domination. The Roman Catholic branch of Christianity, in particular, has taken this very characteristic to an extreme. The roots of the desire for domination were already found in the New Testament with "Pauline Politics," which was later developed into "Augustinian Politics," as was convincingly showed by Roger Garaudy.[2] For Paul, the power of God, of Christ, of faith and of the resurrection, and obedience to political power are structural elements of the main institutions of our world. In Augustine, the divine sphere maintains its supremacy over the sphere of humankind, and the latter must always subjugate itself to the former. Within this historical context and with the support of these two great men – St. Paul and St. Augustine – who helped shape Christianity, the category of power became axial to the structure of the official organization of Christianity. It is around the Sacred power that the hierarchy of the Church is structured, a hierarchy that claims to have the monopoly of knowledge and of what is spoken by and decided in communities. This power that is held by these hierarchies has always worked with the power held by other dominant groups. Because of the alliance between these groups, one cannot write the history of the Church without at the same time referring to the history of Christian kings and princes, and vice versa.

In the same way, Christian missionary activity around the world was also strongly linked to the expansionist and imperialist projects of the Christian Western powers. It was usual for conquest and missionary work to constitute the same project, and an instance of this is the case of Latin America and of a number of countries in Africa. As a direct consequence of this, wherever Christianity arrived in those places it brought with it the destruction of the native religions and it imposed the Western understanding of faith and way of life. It is for this very reason that the majority of those who live outside the Western world think of Christianity as the religion of conquerors and that it partakes of cruelty and irreverence. Christianity was accomplice to genocides and ethnocides, the effects of which are still being felt by many to this date. This is made even more regrettable by the fact that official and hierarchic Christianity, especially the Roman Catholic denomination, does not show any sort of willingness to acknowledge its historical responsibility and to beg forgiveness from the victims of such acts; evidence for this was seen in the 4th Conference of Latin American Bishops in San Domingo in 1992 and in the various official celebrations of the 500th Anniversary of Latin America in Spain and various other countries. This is a very arrogant and merciless attitude. Even the call for forgiveness by Pope John Paul II with respect to the crimes against Jews and to the victims of the Inquisition met strong resistance within the Vatican central apparatus. This call for forgiveness of Pope John Paul II, however, only refers to victims of the past, never referring to the current victims of the church; it does not refer to victims of his harsh ecclesiastical policies of silencing bishops and censuring dozens of theologians while at the head of the Vatican.

This dominating character of Christianity showed itself both in its missionary activities to other lands and also in the homeland where it influenced the relations between churchgoers. It is characterized by a strong centralization and sanctification of power, by the subordination of all who are not part of the hierarchical structure, and by marginalizing and excluding women. This kind of Christianity is part of the Western world; it thinks, it organizes itself and it communicates itself in a Western manner; and, as such, it cannot be universal. It creates the standardization of itself by ways of imposition, such as happened during the Romanization of Catholicism across the whole world, or with the obvious manipulation of the Latin American bishops and of the texts produced by these in San Domingos by the representatives of Rome, or with the celebration of the synod of African bishops in Rome, instead of a more appropriate African venue. This kind of Christianity belongs to a culture of domination. As such powerful criticisms must be leveled against it, so that it does not undermine the process of globalization, which is often confused with Westernization. The manipulation of Christianity by groups who pursue interests of supremacy and domination must be denounced since this is in contradiction to the original Christian ideal.

The more official Christianity re-inforces its mechanisms for subjugating all to the power of the hierarchies; the more it re-affirms its dogmatism, controls the doctrines, imposes its liturgy and shows itself as having the higher moral ground, the more it shows its Western face, and thus, the more fallible it shows itself, the more incapable of stimulating hope and of communicating to those who are outside its sphere of influence. It is a victim of its own doings; it is a victim of its parochial mentality that tries to universalize itself in the insane or pathological format of the standardization of everything or of the imposition of a particular idea to all cultures. This strategy does not support the globalization of humanity and spirituality; rather, it hinders the rise of the new civilization.

It must be noted, however, that the history of Christianity also has other important elements, such as prophecy and the missionary work that abandons the matrix of power and puts itself at the service of the poor. This alternative approach has always been present in the history of Christianity and it has been particularly represented by the religious orders and congregations, such as the desert monks of the fourth century, the Benedictine, the Mendicant, the Franciscan, the Dominican, the Carmelite and Servites traditions of the Middle Ages and the Brothers and Sisters of Jesus and the special relationship of the churches linked to the liberation theology in the Third World with the poor. The missionary work done within this context is not done to implement the Western characteristics of the Church; rather it is done as a call of the gospel to the brotherhoods of monks and sisterhoods of nuns who put themselves at the service of other people within the context of the local culture and thus creating a synthesis of religious faith and the actual life of churchgoers. This is the Christianity of liberation, which is so beneficial to the process of globalization exactly because it renounces the mechanisms of domination and appreciates the uniqueness of each cultural expression as well as the possible communication between all these different cultures, and as such this kind of Christianity is an important factor in constructing a proper and universalized reality.

Faith Can be Universalized, the Christian Religion Can Not

The process of globalization and the crisis in organized Christianity lead us back to paleo-Christianity, that is, to the Christian faith. Faith always implies a profound encounter with the Mystery that inhabits this world and that religions and scholars have deciphered as being God. The religious experience can be expressed in various manners and its account can never be exhausted. Thus, it can be told in various languages and manners throughout the ages. Religious experience is, due to its very nature, universal, exactly because it is an experience open to all, that is to say, it is trans-cultural and occurs everywhere and at all times. For this very reason faith unites and creates communities. The variations of this faith, however, are always related to a particular culture, place and time, and as such they show differences.

When a religion naïvely identifies itself with faith, forgetting that it is a particular variation of faith, it excludes all those who subscribe to a different version of this faith. This is a fundamentalist understanding of faith. Under this particular light, differences create divisions, and divisions lead to religious wars. Hence, faith, the religious experience of the Mystery of the world, is not the reason for divisions among humanity; rather, religions, the interpretations of faith that identify themselves as being faith, are. Official Christianity has, by and large, committed this mistake. It has identified faith with Christian religion, Christ's Church with the Roman Catholic Church, the ability to perform a religious act with hierarchical power, and Christianity with the Western world. In order to correct this deficiency it is important to go back to the original ideals of Christianity, the ideals held before Christianity became founded in sacred power and in hierarchical communities. In doing so, Christianity can be of service to the process of globalization and help with the rise of the global civilization.

The Christian faith, and since it followed from the Jewish, I should say the Judaeo-Christian faith, manifests itself primarily as an utopia. Utopia does not oppose or contradict reality. It belongs to reality as it expresses potentialities of the reality that have not yet been realized.

The utopia envisaged by the Judaeo-Christian tradition is the following: there exists a global and ultimate sense of reality; everything is destined to preserve itself in being, to achieve self-fulfillment and to transfigure itself. Death will not have the last word, life will, and life will occur in abundance. This joyful event is the gift of God to his creation, to his sons and daughters, who because of their own creativity are able to be co-creators of God's creation.

This is represented in the covenant that God forged between himself and all living beings, a covenant that is symbolized by the rainbow – this is the covenant of Noah and it is found in Genesis 9:11. The covenant with Israel was forged to promote the understanding that each nation is a nation of God – this is found in Genesis 12:3. And lastly, the covenant of love and of the blood of Christ, which brings liberation by making us all feel like sons and daughters of God – this is found in Luke 22:20 and Romans 8:29. Hence, covenants do not possess any tribal or one-sided meaning, as it can sometimes be portrayed by an ideology that understands that only some have been chosen. Historically, the tribal or one-sided reading of covenants has been used to justify so many cases of prejudice against, and the massacre of, people. The covenant is always with the whole; it covers, just like the rainbow, all nations of the Earth and Earth as a whole. If it has started as covering only one nation or community, it is because its destiny is to surpass itself and encompass the whole.

The expression "Kingdom of God," which is a recurrent and important theme in Jesus' preaching, is related to this covenant with the whole. The Kingdom of God is not a territory; it is rather an expression of being or a situation in which justice reigns, mercy is in place, love governs, life triumphs and the feeling of God flourishes in people and in the whole of creation.

The utopia of a Kingdom materializes itself in history, but it has its apex in God itself. It always starts with the weakest link. The Kingdom first materializes itself in beings who are in danger and in the human beings who are more oppressed and marginalized. It is for this very reason that the Kingdom has an unmistakable emancipatory dimension: "Happy are you poor; the Kingdom of God is yours!" (Luke 6:20).

This utopia gains an historical embodiment in all things that preserve, defend and promote life. The subject of life is a very central theme in the Judeao-Christian tradition. God is a living, creating and fulfilling God. In the scriptures life is a determination, a willpower, of all beings; in a manner of speaking, they live because they are made alive by the breath of the creator (*Spiritus Creator*), are under the benevolent eye of God and are cared for and loved by him. It is for this very reason that the heaven, the stones, the mountains, the gales, the plants and the animals demonstrate the glory of God. With life comes justice, mercy and love.

Kingdom – the meaning of meanings, the supreme value of all creation – is freedom *from* and freedom *to*. It is the liberation from everything that breaks the covenant of co-living and solidarity between beings and also liberation from the gap that distances God. It is liberty for all that regains the original direction and for all that brings qualitative and quantitative evolution to the whole of creation.

Lastly, an element of hope, the resurrection of the body, belongs to the Judeao-Christian faith. Resurrection is much more than the mere reanimation of a corpse. It is the fulfillment and the transfiguration of all and every being. I mean, what was merely a potential of reality, now becomes sheer reality; what was a written promise in the dynamism of all creation, now is fully achieved. It is the world regressing to its very source in a more intense and complete manner, and thus "fulfilling" God himself. The resurrection of the Crucified constitutes the first rehearsal and free sample of what is to come to each of us and to the whole universe.

The certainty of the Christian faith and hope can be expressed in any language. Faith does not exclude anything. It lifts things up and pushes things forward. It is universal because of its promise of hope, its support for creation and the possibilities it opens up. It reaffirms the meaning of life, the complexity and unity of the universe, and the ultimate destiny of life in the life of God himself.

This same faith has been expressed in all cultures, in the plurality of religions and of experiencing the Divine and the Sacred. No culture has a monopoly on its experiencing and expressing. All cultures are relative and open. This does not make faith itself something relative; it only makes the experiencing of the faith relative to the various cultural expressions of it. When we know and we respect the differences, we are enriched by the uniqueness of the faith that is common to all, a faith that possesses a personal, common, cosmic and divine dimension.

This is the Christianity of Liberation since it connects itself to the other expressions of faith without patronising them, and as such, it does not oppress or destroy them. It realizes the dream of Jesus and of all sincere religious persons; we are not going to worship God in Gerizim, nor in Jerusalem, nor in Rome, nor in Mecca; rather, we are going to worship him in spirit and truth as *per* John 4:23, and, as such, in all places and circumstances. There will be more spirit and truth through the extent to which worship is connected to a commitment to the liberation of the oppressed and the excluded of history and of nature. This is the kind of liturgy that is agreeable to God (cf. Micah 6:7 and Matthew 23:23) exactly because it recovers the union of the human family, the family of God. It provides the conditions for human beings to be free and able to have friendly and loving relationships.

6 Conclusion to Part I: Fidelity to the Greatest of Dreams

To give birth to a child is always a difficult and dangerous experience. The baby faces the worst experience of his or her life as it is squeezed from all sides, finally being expelled from the mother's belly. The new always comes about in an analogous fashion. Humanity is currently facing a difficult transition. It moves from the national to the global, from the global to the cosmic. It moves from mass and energy to information and communication. It moves from the macro to the micro (the miniaturization of devices and machinery), from the visible to the invisible (nuclear energy and leisure); from an externality to an internality, from a materialism to a holistic spiritualism, from a linear form of reasoning to a dialectical form of reasoning that understands the complexities of reality. This Passover, this journey, is not without some glitches and some substantial grief; some contradictions between the old that insist on remaining and the new that persists in flourishing. However, just as the mother who is in labor is joyful despite her enduring pains, we also are joyful because a new child is going to be born, a global humanity more human and benevolent.

I maintain the thesis that great changes are at our doors, that a new global civilization will emerge, and that we are moving towards a convergent communication between consciousnesses, namely, a noosphere. This noosphere would mean the fitting together of the human mind to the current phenomena of globalization, or better said, it would be the manifestation of the phenomena of globalization/unification of the world in the human mind. The human mind is also part of the process.

Human beings have this unique characteristic within creation. Human beings are co-pilots of nature in the process of creation. We can slow down the process or even divert it sometimes. However, it is not in our power to halt the passage of time or the evolution of the universe. This would be to underestimate them. Human beings can help or disturb the process of evolution, a process that has taken place over billions of years. Blaise Pascal described very well the human condition in his *Pensées* when he says: "this feeble thing...this novelty...monster...chaos...subject of contradictions, prodigy, judge of all things, stupid worm of the earth, holder of truth, pit of uncertainties and errors, glory and leftover of the universe."[1] Human beings are, however, responsible for their actions and as such they are the only ethical beings in the whole of creation.

It is the responsibility of human beings to devise the link that connects and reconnects everything. This challenge is met by religion. Religion seeks to reconnect everything, the conscious with the unconscious, the mind with the body, a person with the world, the masculine with the feminine, and the human with the divine. The task of religion is neither fulfilled nor exhausted in the sacred sphere. Its place is in life where it must do this re-connection and synthesis. When this is successful, God is experienced; and religion then is experienced as the thread that passes through everything and that unifies, uplifts and takes things forward. In such a way the symbols and the rituals that constitute the sacred sphere, and in which the God of life, of the community, of humanity and of the cosmos is celebrated, are created.[2]

This re-connection is felt through the religious experience, as I described previously. The challenge to religions, particularly Christianity, is to go back to the kind of faith that brings with it a fulfilling experience and thus re-establishing the re-connection between everything. Nowadays, this is an urgent challenge due to the accelerated process of the unification of human-ity. This faith must develop a commitment to social justice so that the two-thirds of humanity, who find themselves excluded, can be introduced into the human family. For this very reason, faith will either be emancipatory or it will re-connect nothing.

The mission of re-connection is a mission for all and each of us. Christianity can stimulate in people its responsibility to maintain the dream of a world that is reconciled and just, in a cosmos that is counting on us to achieve a higher level of complexity, interiority, and unification just as has been occurring for billions of years; and it must also provide a proper and coherent example to all.

It is important that each of us engage in small changes wherever we are. We must not leave such actions to the care of others; we must act ourselves. There is no impossible task; we can bring changes to a group, a community, a church or to a nation. Each of us is in a position to implement change.

Only by acting in this manner can the forces of the *homo sapiens* be capable of balancing out the forces of the *homo demens* and thus achiev-ing another step towards its immersion in the universe and towards the encounter with that Mystery of tenderness and happiness that inheres in the universe and that wishes a free and conscious relation between human beings.

Part II
The New World Order and Christianity

Does Christianity help Humanity towards the New Millennium?

On one thing we can all agree, South and North: we are currently living a great crisis. It is a crisis in civilization; by this, I mean a crisis of the global meaning of our existence in this world.

How does Christianity help humanity to overcome this crisis, so that we can begin the 21st century with greater hope for the future?

7 The World Crisis from the Ethical and Political Perspective of the South

From what kind of perspective are we to tackle this crisis? I am strongly convinced that this crisis must be tackled from an ethical perspective, and not from a merely political one. It is important to make use of a perspective with principles. The perspective with principles is the one that allows reality to reveal itself; and as such, it is the one that does not conceal reality from those large numbers of people who are suffering, are desperate and dying before their time. This ethical perspective is the one that is currently being politically developed in the South, where two-thirds of humanity live, and are being crucified, and who are partners of those who live in the rich countries of the North.

This ethical perspective, however, is just the starting point. For the final stage, for the global solution, we need to incorporate the perspectives of those who live in countries of the Northern hemisphere. In this manner we can combine ethics with politics.

What is the situation of humanity in the South? The data is well known:

- More than a billion people (three times more than the whole population of the European Union) live in absolute poverty, living on less than a dollar a day.
- More than two billion people have only two dollars a day to attend to all their necessities.
- About 900 million adults are illiterate.
- About two billion people do not have access to drinking water.
- 100 million people (the equivalent of the combined populations of France, Spain and Belgium put together) are homeless.
- 800 million people live in a state of famine.
- 150 million children, up to the age of five years old, suffer from malnutrition.
- 14 million children die annually before they are five days' old.[1]

Other international organizations, such as the IMF and the World Bank, have similar reports.

The international debt of the poor countries in the 1990s was about one trillion and 300 billion dollars. Between 1980 and 1990 there was a great influx of capital of about 450 billion dollars from the poor to the rich countries. This is the equivalent of two complete Marshall Plans, the plan that re-built Europe after the Second World War. In this way, one can easily understand the reasons why the rich countries have tripled their wealth while cutting down on working hours by a quarter in the last 30 years.

In the 1980s and 1990s the countries in Latin America have transferred to the rich countries about two hundred billion dollars as payment to service the interest of their national debts; these are debts that amounted to four hundred billion dollars in total.

Who helps whom? The world is upside down. The poor help the rich. The rich countries do not need to invest any more in technically underdeveloped countries. It is enough to collect payments for the poor countries' national debts. The wealth and exports of poor countries are given as an advanced guarantee for payments of their national debts. The situation gets even worse due to the process of globalization that occurs under the banner of global financing.

Without a doubt we are currently experiencing an advanced process of globalization through the economy, science and technology, communication, informatics and cultural trends. We are increasingly doing away with the important word *development*, and replacing it with the word *market*, and with the integration of continental markets in the world market. The flavor of the moment for all heads of state is *modernization* or *modernity*.

What is behind these words *modernization* and *modernity*? A new social ideology is behind it, a new ideology that is trying to replace the words capitalism and socialism. What is the path towards modernization? The answer: *neo-liberalism*! Neo-liberalism has been considered by some as the apex of history, and by others the end of history itself. For this very reason, countries have felt forced to achieve modernization by neo-liberal ways.

But, what is neo-liberalism? And what does it want to achieve? Let us spell it out clearly and in so many words: it is the current phase of accumulative capitalism. The basis of production is not national or trans-national any more; rather, it is global. This is achieved by the use of the most advanced and environmentally friendly technology available, which only the countries in the North possess and which are not released to developing countries.

Its core value is privatization and consequently it is a tribute to the individual. There is pressure for the state to minimize its overall role. The state must invest less in social areas, health, education, and social security. To propose such a thing to the countries of the South is to condemn millions of poor people to death. Why? Because the majority of these countries have not yet implemented enough changes in society. In these countries the state is the sole provider of health, education, housing, and public services. No private company in those countries invests in social benefits without gaining something in return.

The 1980s are considered by the countries in the Third World as a decade that was lost forever, with no progress. According to the Food and Agriculture Organization of the United Nations the top five percent of the richest people in Latin America have increased their wealth by eight percent in the past ten years; while the bottom 75 percent of the poorest people became 13 percent less well off. That is to say, the gap between rich and poor has got wider by 21 percent.

The international financial institutions and the governments of the countries of the North have imposed on the countries of the South a policy known as *structural adjustments*. Through these structural changes the national economies must adapt to the demands of a market that is dominated by the core capitalist countries.

This market economy is presented as the ultimate reality, as the most natural thing, and as the only way forward for global production. I am not necessarily against the market economy. However, this integrated capitalist market has some particularities that bring with it perverse consequences. This market requires *competition*, which in turn has a form of reasoning that aims at excluding competitors from the market. Only companies and nations that use the most up-to-date technologies, that are not released to other companies and nations, are competitive. The stronger ones hold these technologies that are responsible for modernization, which brings with it development and profits. There is no solidarity and international cooperation here.

In neo-liberalism one finds the logic of exclusion, exactly because it is based on modernization and competition. The countries of the South are not interesting any more because they hold technology that is dated. They are not competitive and have internal political crises because of the dire poverty in which many of their citizens live. It is because of these facts that there are very few foreign investments in the countries of the South. The South is not worth anything because it is outside the market. If one is outside the market one does not exist.

Previously, from the 1960s to the 1980s, there was a kind of economic policy that aimed at development. The South was under-developed and it desired to develop itself. The South was confronted by the system and desired either its place within the system or to transform the system. In those days there was optimism and hope.

Now prevails the kind of economic policy that only aims at paying the international debts of these countries. These payments consume between 35 to 50 percent of Third World countries' incomes. The South is poorer than it used to be. There is no more hope. There is no more hope in finding the solution to traditional problems within this current economic system. The South finds itself excluded. And the excluded are not confronted by the system, since they are excluded from it; rather, they are faced by dire poverty, are marginalized and confronted by death. In many places flourishes a culture of disillusion and despair.

There is a propagation of the idea that the countries of the so-called Third World, the world that represents two-thirds of humanity, has neither future nor salvation. If these countries want to be acknowledged they must subjugate themselves to the economic and social policies of the core countries. They must obey the mentality of globalization. The overall effect on these poor countries' populations is more iniquitous than the effects of colonization.

Globalization brings with it standardization. Across the world one finds the same values for a global system, the same cultural trends and the same manner of consuming. The virulence of this market is destroying unprotected cultures. Everything becomes tediously the same in the city center of Rio, Mexico City, the center of Prague, just like the center of Paris, the center of New York and the center of Berlin.

When in 1989 the first McDonald's restaurant opened in Moscow a representative said: "We have the credit for creating the Big Mac. It is the same in Rio, in New York, in Tokyo, in Peking, in Singapore, and now here in Moscow." It is the same kind of bread, meat and tomato sauce. It is the same recipe and the same taste. This case exemplifies the reasoning behind the system of globalization, the reasoning of standardization.

Globalization transforms everything in a kind of homogeneous Big Mac. We see the same kind of style for hotels, dress, films, music, and television programs. Even the Vatican has its own Big Mac. It created a unique catechism for the whole world. This catechism is the same, with the same sins and virtues, whether you are in the North Pole, in the tropics of the Amazon rainforest, in Rome, in Bangkok or in Tahiti. This is the glorious catholic Big Mac.

It is easy to become convinced that there is no alternative to this model of society. As shown by the economic studies of Franz Hinkelammert, who writes from the perspective of the Great South, any alternative becomes impossible because it does not possess enough vigor to support itself, and especially because the current powers do not want or have the power to undermine any alternative system (cf. the case of Nicaragua and the economic blockade of Cuba).

8 The Roots of the World Crisis

The current crisis is an extreme one; it is a crisis that questions the basic fundamentals of our culture. In abstract terms it means a crisis that questions our current paradigm. In concrete terms it expresses a crisis of the dream and of the ideology that has guided the world for centuries. What kind of dream was this? This was the dream of unlimited development, a willingness to achieve power and dominate other people, other nations and nature itself.

More than the *cogito, ergo sum*, or "I think therefore I am," of Descartes is the *conquero, ergo sum*, or "I conquer, therefore I am," of Hernán Cortez, who conquered and destroyed the original populations of Mexico. This expresses well the dynamics of modernity. The popes of the time, Nicolas V (1447–1455) and Alexander (1492–1503) granted divine legitimacy to the European attitude of domination. In the name of God it was given to the imperialist powers of the time, the kingdoms of Spain and Portugal, "the full power and liberty to invade, conquer, combat, triumph and submit the pagans, and to seize for themselves and use for their own benefit the lands, possessions and goods belonging to these pagans... Because His Divine Majesty agrees that the barbaric nations must be reduced and brought over to the Christian faith."[1]

Descartes and Francis Bacon, masters of the modern paradigm, said the same thing as the popes: the human being is the "master and owner of nature" and he must "overcome nature and force her to give up her secrets; he must put nature to his services as a slave."

What is all this for? For our development and happiness. Science and technology are the great weapons in the project of domination of nations and nature and in the creation of conditions for the development and happiness of the European.

The Paradigm of Modernity within Capitalism and Socialism

The paradigm of modernity expressed itself in two opposing social systems, namely, capitalism and socialism.

Capitalism privatized all goods and assets and socialized dreams. Socialism socialized all goods and assets and privatized dreams. Explaining this further, capitalism privatized all goods and assets. In other words, industries, land and banks become private properties. But it allowed dreams to be expressed through the means of communication, especially through advertising and television. Capitalism allows the socialization of dreams as long as it is socialized within the parameters imposed by the interests of capital. In a shanty town there may be lack of food, but it will have a TV set. The TV feeds the dreams through advertising, soap operas and communicative images.

Socialism socialized the goods, lands, industries, and education. But it privatized the dreams. Only the dreams that were either dreamt by the single governing party or in accordance with the sole socialist dream were accepted. All other dreams were repressed or persecuted.

Today we can tally the outcome of these systems.

Socialism failed. By forbidding dreams, it hindered freedom and creativity and as such it destroyed its humanitarian sense. It imploded.

Capitalism allows dreams. Dreams, even when mistaken, support hope and prolong life. For this very reason capitalism has survived. These dreams, however, only live in images…

And for this very reason also, capitalism did not solve any of the problems that socialism proposed to resolve. On the contrary, the problems have worsened on a global level. Today we find that there is much more poverty and violence than before, in both rich and poor countries.

What is the irony in this? After 500 years of living the dream of development we find that this very dream caused the under-development of the majority of countries in the world. The domination of nature provoked her rebellion, threatening the life of human beings and other species with pollution, the hole in the ozone layer and other ecological imbalances.

The modern paradigm of power implemented as the domination of the world and nations has yielded three main anomalies that profoundly mark our globalized culture: the simplification of the concept of human beings, the repression of the feminine and the disrespect of differences and of nature.

The Simplification of the Concepts of Human Beings and Society

What kind of concept of human being is behind the dream of development and material prosperity?

It is the concept of a human being as a being that has needs. Experience and the ancient philosophies tell us that the needs of human beings are unlimited. It follows that in order to satisfy these unlimited needs, development must also be limitless. As it happens, those needs can never be fully satisfied. And thus, as long as human beings guide themselves by following their needs, there will be frustration. Will nature cope with this procedure?

Let us remind ourselves here of Gandhi who said: "the Earth can provide for the basic necessities of all human beings, but it cannot cope with the voracity of consumers."

Well, human beings are not merely beings that have needs, unlike animals. Human beings do not only hunger for bread; they also have hunger for beauty, communion and achievement. In short, a human being is a social, benevolent and spiritual being. They are able to take care of the world and to show affection to other human beings. They also have higher dreams; they have dreams of absolute love and of losing themselves in the wider picture of things. They dream with God. They are not condemned to be chained to their needs, like an animal; rather they are free beings and companions of other human beings.

The meaning of life portrayed by modernity did not fully integrate these features in the concept of human beings. This is the reason why we are currently facing a crisis concerning our identity, our hopes and our future.

The Repression of the Feminine

Another element, among various others, that has caused the current crisis we are living in is the repression of the feminine. By feminine it is not meant women. Feminine and masculine are components of each human being, man and woman. Feminine and masculine are two principles, two forces, that construct and constitute the human being, man and woman. The feminine is the principle of interiority, of care, of respect of life and of the Mystery of the world, that all of us must develop in ourselves. Women do this in their own manner. But men are also able to fulfill this principle in their own way.

As it happens, modern culture is founded on power. The will for power has repressed the feminine principle in men, in women, in society and in religions. This is a culture of working away from home, of exteriority, of the use of power to dominate relations between human beings and between human beings and nature.

For these reasons we have a scientific approach that is aggressive and chauvinist, a society that is fundamentally masculine and churches that are misogynous. Thus, we find the motive for our current bland lifestyle; a lifestyle that does not glow with any *anima*. Moreover, it is noteworthy here that women are the great victims of this kind of lifestyle.

Women constitute more than half of humanity and are the sisters and mothers of the other half of humankind, men. How sane is a society that is founded on violence between people, in the aggression against nature and in the marginalization of women?

The Disrespect of Differences and of Nature

Humanity encompasses differences such as gender, races, cultures, opinions, ways of relating to nature and religions.

How did Western culture, that is so dominating, behave in the face of so many differences? The answer is, in an atrocious manner. Westerners have great difficulty in living with differences. With very few exceptions the Western strategy was the following: whenever in contact with Africans, Asians, indigenous populations, non-whites, make use of force. The strategy was to dominate them, assimilate them, so that they would become similar to Westerners. Otherwise the strategy was to destroy them. Rarely was an alliance forged with the different so that humanity could progress together in this great adventure that is life.

The relation between Europeans and the original Latin American cultures in the 16th century was dramatic. The non-acceptance of the different caused the biggest genocide in the history of humankind. In one single century, 50 million people were killed, or died as a consequence of the violence, during the conquest.

Disrespect also impinges on the other great otherness that is nature. Nature is not welcomed for its self-sufficiency, for its inherent value, and for being independent of human beings; it existed for millions of years before the *homo* species first appeared. Earth and nature are thus reduced to a conglomeration of resources which are at the disposal of greedy human beings, who think of themselves as being the masters of these. The level of degradation in the quality of life is so obvious that it can do without any further considerations.

The question now is this: is it possible to sustain an unlimited development and at the same time avoid the devastation of nature and the increase of misery in the world?

9   Towards a New Alliance

In order for us to overcome this crisis we must elaborate a new dream and articulate a new meaning of life. In religious terminology, we would say that we need a new spirituality, a new encounter with the Being that brings with it an inner meaning to life and to history and that deciphers the Mystery of the world, the reason for evolution, and the passage of time. In short, we need a new encounter with Being as the original source of all things.

The Paradigm of Re-connection

There is a need for a new religion, a new religion in the original and ety-mological sense of the word. That is to say, there is a need for something to re-connect everything in the widest sense so that it can serve a thread that can sew together all experiences, all knowledge, all spiritual traditions, all politics, all humanity, and help us forge a new global reality that is united, diverse, dynamic and inclusive. In order to do this, we must dialectically put together and integrate all the various elements, and identify the com-plexities involved in this; once this is done, a new progressive outcome can arise within a convergent perspective. Politically it is important, for instance, to learn the lessons of the political systems of the past in a synthe-sis that is human and spiritual.

Capitalism created the culture of the *I without the We*. Socialism created the culture of the *We without the I*. Now we need to synthesis these systems so that we can create the kind of living that enables the *I with the We*. We need neither individualism nor collectivism; rather, we need a social and participative democracy. We need to do some corrections to our conception of human being so that it integrates the feminine and an alliance with nature. Only then can a new spirituality appear that re-connects everything.

Human Beings as Social Beings

Perhaps the best definition of a human being is the following: human beings are a knot of relations that stretches in all directions. This implies that a human being is a person, that is, he or she is a being that is open to give and receive, to participation, to solidarity, and to communion. All these terms demonstrate that the path followed by a human being is a two-way road. The more human beings communicate, reach out, and give a bit of themselves, the more they receive from their fellow human beings, and the more human, the more personal, they are.

Therefore, when a human being is understood as a knot of relations it turns the human being into a subject, "I," that is at the same time within a community, "we."

This human fact must be expressed politically. We need to go beyond socialism and capitalism if we want to live in community, construct a social and participative democracy that is bottom to top and that includes all. These are perhaps the key words in the political world-scene nowadays: social and participative democracy. This political system supports itself on four pillars as noted by Herbert de Souza (who is well-known in Brazil as Betinho), as follows:

- *Participation*: Human beings are rational and free. A human being does not want to be a mere assistant or beneficiary; rather, he wants to be a participant agent, an actor, of the collective project. Only this enables him to become a subject in history. Such participation must be done bottom to top so that nobody is excluded.
- *Equality*: Equality is achieved through the participation of all. The more one participates in everything that happens, the more one builds up equality. Each of us is singular and different. Participation, however, stops differences from becoming inequalities. This is equality in dignity and rights, an equality that supports social justice. With the search for equality comes equity, that is, my share for my cooperation in society.
- *Differences*: Differences must be respected and welcomed as a manifestation of the potentialities of people and cultures and as a great source of modes of participation. Differences reveal all the riches of the same and unique humanity.
- *Communion*: Human beings possess subjectivity, the capacity of communicating with their inner being and with the subjectivity of other human beings. Human beings have values, are able to feel compassion and solidarity with the weak, and can dialogue with nature and with the divine. This is spirituality.

These four pillars together constitute our dream of a communal, participative, harmonious and spiritual humankind. They teach us to link one's personal desires and wants to collective desires and wants.

This participative and social democracy opens itself to a cosmic dimension, and this is necessary because we cannot exist without the community of life, our environment. The other beings of nature are linked to our existence. They also have rights. And as such they must be included, as co-citizens, in the socio-cosmic democracy. In this way, the commonwealth of human beings will also be a commonwealth of nature and of all forms of life.

The Integration of the Feminine in Men and Women

This kind of encompassing democracy will provide the opportunity for integrating the feminine principle in people and in culture. Rationality, efficiency and labor must not be the only important things in life. Benevolence, tenderness, attention to life, a co-living full of joy and the respect of all things should also be considered important in life. These latter points are part of the feminine dimension that is expressed in men and women.

Women will be in a state of equality with men. Together, men and women in partnership, each with their own differences, will take on the totality of their tasks within the family and in public life. It will be the person, and not the gender, that will serve as reference.

Because of a more active participation of women in public life, there will be more care, tenderness and protection of life and for the life of the weak or penalized by nature and by history. Because chauvinism will be a thing of the past, and because of the integration of the feminine in the conception of human beings, there will certainly be fewer conflicts which lead to the destabilization of the relations between human beings and between human beings and the cosmos. There will be more possibilities for peace.

A New Alliance with Nature

Human beings increasingly discover themselves as part of nature, a member of the community of life. The relation between a human being and nature cannot be a relation of domination; rather, it must be a relation of co-living in an alliance of fraternity, respect and dialogue. Human beings require nature to provide for their needs, and at the same time, nature, which has been marked by human cultures, needs human beings so that it can be preserved, maintained and able to recover its equilibrium. All beings in nature are subjects with rights, because, in their own way, they are carriers of information and of subjectivity. On this ground, everything that exists and lives deserves to exist and live.

As I have mentioned above, democracy cannot apply only to human beings and society, it also needs to apply to the cosmos. What would society be without trees, clear waters, fresh air, and the brightness of the stars? Human beings must understand all these entities as citizens also. Human beings must feel linked, as brother and sister, to all beings in the universe. This cosmological outlook will open up the possibility for a new experiencing of the Sacred and the Divine that sustains the universe and that religions call God.

Departing from this new alliance, which is founded in the common-wealth of both human beings and the cosmos, we must redefine the path for social changes.

Until recently we were directed by the dream of great redeeming revolutions: the technological and scientific revolution, the bourgeois revolution, the socialist revolution, the cybernetic revolution. All of these revolutions required a vast amount of human and ecological sacrifices. Millions of people, a vast amount of wealth and of cultural assets were sacrificed and lost forever. Today, by and large, the majority of people have lost their belief in great revolutions that may be applied to all societies.

We do require revolutions, however, so that the necessary changes are implemented. These revolutions will not have their origins in political powers, which presuppose a particular historical approach, a specific project and a strategy of implementation. The age for these kinds of revolution is gone. In the current phase of globalization, we require a coalition of ethical, moral and humanitarian forces that mobilize themselves to implement changes that are focused on the destiny of all humanity. These changes begin with the transformations of personal and collective subjectivities.

We believe in the small changes. Just as molecules, which are the small parts of life matter, guarantee their lives through the relation and communication that they maintain with other molecules and with the environment, in a similar manner revolutions must start in the groups and communities that have interest in changes. In these groups one finds the opportunity to change people, the group's actions, and the relations of the group with its immediate society. From this one can move to higher spheres of society.

These small revolutions are currently in place all around the world; we see everywhere in the world the setting up of groups, communities and organizations that have a fraternal approach to the oppressed and marginalized of the system. These are groups that are concerned with the problems of the environment and with indigenous populations; these are groups that support initiatives to help those who are helping themselves and that have a preference in acquiring produce from poor countries; these are groups that experience a new spirituality and religion. There is an exchange of experiences between groups of rich countries with groups of poor countries; they visit each other and discuss new common ideas of globalization that are not founded on the market, on the economy and on techno-science; rather, these new common ideas of globalization are founded in solidarity, in the open exchange of ideas and in learning from each other.

We find ourselves slowly going back to our common fatherland. Everywhere is emerging a more benevolent and respectful relation with nature. We have started to co-live with the mountains, the jungles, animals, birds, and nature's other elements as benevolent brothers and sisters, who share a common destiny. Slowly there emerges a better approach to development, an approach to social development that is centered on the poor and others who are excluded from the system.

The poor and the excluded are the carriers of a new dream. They are in all quarters of the planet. The important thing here is to strongly believe in the redeeming powers of this dream of a common destiny.

10 How Much does Christianity Help with the Construction of the 21st Century?

How does Christianity help the task of redefining the sense of human beings living together? What kind of contribution can it make to a spirituality that encompasses the other spiritual traditions of humanity? How can it help to create a new meaning of life?

Before proceeding, we must acknowledge, as many theologians have already accepted, that Christianity is partly responsible for the current crisis. Christianity has enforced with practices, biblical texts and doctrines the idea of human beings as masters and conquerors of creation.

The form by which Christianity organized itself socially also influenced this crisis. That is, by centralizing the power in the hands of clergy and excluding the women and marginalizing the laymen from sharing in this power, this makes Christianity partly responsible, not solely responsible, for the current crisis. The South still perceives Christianity as being too Eurocentric, Western, excluding and not-universalized.

The gesture of Ramiro Reynaga, a native Indian chief in Bolivia, at the time of the visit of the Pope to his country in 1985, is very symbolic for a school of thought that is critical of organized Christianity. Reynaga gave a letter to the Pope in the name of all native Indians which said: "We, native Indians of the Andes and of America, decide to take this occasion to give back to you your Bible because in five centuries it gave us neither love, nor peace, nor justice. Please, your Holiness, take your Bible back and pass it on to our oppressors because they have more need of its moral lessons than we do." Since the arrival of Christopher Columbus a culture, language, religion and values that are particular to Europe was imposed with force on the Americas. The Spanish sword that during the day attacked and murdered the body of native Indians, during the night transformed itself into the Cross that attacked their souls. The pope said nothing. He had a most dignifying attitude: he cried.

Organized Christianity finds itself committed to the culture of domination. And for this reason we cannot hold our hopes up. This can be clearly seen in the centers of the Church, especially the Vatican, which have a strategy that aims at the neo-Romanization of all the Church, the establishment of parameters for the council of Bishops, the control of any alternative theology, the homogenization of doctrines in a universal catechism, and with other measures of centralization of power. They want a strong Christianity in the Americas and in Africa that is dependent on Europe. It must be noted, however, that there is another kind of Christianity other than this official or organized strain. There is also a community-based Christianity.

Within community-based Christianity there are a number of figures, groups, organizations and theological schools that attempt to recoup the original dream of Jesus. They envisage a new paradigm for Christianity, a new paradigm that is beneficial to humanity and to nature.

There are three elements within the various perspectives of the Judaeo-Christian tradition that enable us to enter the 21st century with more hope. These are: the logic of inclusion, the new alliance, and the strength of the weak. This trinity is a response to the three fundamental challenges posed by the current status quo. And as such these elements must be within the new spirituality.

The Logic of the Inclusion of All

There is an awful fact in our current reality that challenges human rationality and the meaning of Christianity: two-thirds of humanity are literally made up by people who are being crucified. I have already said above that in a global market the vast majority is and feels excluded from this market. This majority finds itself living in dire poverty and facing death.

It is a fact that the poor will not willingly accept the penalty of death, which has been imposed on them by the rich. They will fight back, they will search for benevolence across the world so that they can survive and share humanity's common destiny, a destiny based on justice and life.

Nowadays, if the churches do not take seriously the issue of these people who are being crucified, then I do not understand what they mean when they speak of the Cross, the crucified Jesus, and of the Resurrection of the Crucified. If these churches do not hear the call of those who are oppressed in the world, then how can these churches hear the call of God, the God that the Scriptures describe as the God that calls, the God of life that hears the outcry of the slaves in Egypt, the lamentations of those who are exiled in Babylon, and the wailing of those who suffer?

If we do not assign importance in our reflections and in practicing Christianity to the problems of those who live in dire poverty in the world, then we are not going to save Christianity from its critics and we will be endorsing its historical inappropriateness.

This is unacceptable for a number of reasons. It would be to deprive the poor and the oppressed from a very effective weapon, since Christianity can be a powerful ally of theirs. As a matter of fact, we are disciples of a poor man, a political prisoner, someone who was condemned to death, who was crucified, Jesus of Nazareth.

We must ease the pain of those who are on the cross; we must lower them from the cross, and help them in their resurrection.

But first of all, we must tell these people the good news: if God has a place in this world, then his place is by their very side. God finds himself crucified in the crucified of history. He is in the cross calling for life and resurrection.

It is within this context that we, Christians, must remember our origins as excluded and crucified. As an act of solidarity, we must always recount this historical event. Deuteronomy 26:5 reminds us that "my ancestor was a wandering Aramean." In the first and second millenniums before Christ, Aramean did not designate a nation but individuals in the region of Palestine and Egypt of various origins who were marginalized from the Mesopotamian social structure. These people wandered in search of work. The Hebrew nation was a subgroup at the fringes of this Aramean group. They were enslaved in Egypt. The following passage of Exodus 3:7 refers to them when it states that God says: "I have heard them cry out to be rescued from their slave-drivers... I have come down to rescue them." And God reveals himself as the God of the Hebrew nation in Exodus 20:2: "I am the Lord your God who brought you out of Egypt, where you were slaves." And as such God reveals himself as the God of the excluded and oppressed that yearn for freedom.

The choice of God for the Hebrews of yesterday and of today, and thus, his choice for the excluded, is in direct opposition to the current rationale of exclusion that we find in societies around the world. God starts with the "Hebrews" of all nations; he starts with those who are hopeless in our planet – but he includes us all.

This certainty can ease the cross that is carried by those who are oppressed and who can still have some faith. This certainty can give them hope. God is with them.

More important, however, is to lower them from the cross. We can only lower them from the cross by helping them to build a social and participative democracy, where they can feel that they are persons. This can only be done through the implementation of alternative economic and political policies, as I have argued above. This cannot be done through the kind of politics centered in power and domination; rather, it can only be done through politics focused on benevolent acts and that aim at implementing a human and cosmic commonwealth. We must move from an economy that aims at unlimited growth to an economy that aims to achieve sufficiency and suitability for all. Even after the end of the Cold War, we are still spending three trillion dollars annually in armaments, atomic, biological and chemical weapons. With this amount of money we could provide housing, food, health, education and leisure for all humankind. Why don't we do it?

To lower the oppressed from the cross is very important. More important than this, however, is to create the conditions for resurrection. Resurrecting a nation implies being their partners so that nations can co-live in peace, develop their humanitarian ideals together, express their souls within their cultures, and feel through faith and prayer that these are friends and People of God.

How are we Christians, how are our churches, articulating themselves so that hope is given to the poor? We must consider seriously the choice for the poor. Choosing the poor is to choose the majority of humankind; it is to choose their lives of tragedy and their hopes for the future. The church becomes more true to itself when it chooses to be the church of the poor because it becomes a genuine follower of the poor Jesus. The church becomes an immediate church of the poor in the poor and marginalized. For those who are not poor, but who choose to help the poor, the church becomes as a consequence the church of the poor. In the 21st century 70 percent of Christians will live in the so-called Third World. Thus, it is easy to understand the German theologian, J. B. Metz, who is sympathetic to Liberation Theology, when he says: "The Catholic Church will be, definitely, a Church of the Third World with historical roots in the First World."

Nobody can treat with indifference the life of tragedy of the poor. We are all involved, and for this very reason, when we help the poor, we make ourselves the church of the poor.

The choice for the poor and marginalized constitutes nowadays the very criteria for universalizing, and restoring the credibility of Christianity. In choosing the poor the core churches must become more visionary. These churches must be less concerned with their identity and corporate interests and care more about the common man and woman who have been crucified throughout history. It is through helping them, through presenting their causes to those who formulate social policies and to the public opinion that these churches can build up their identities.

For Christians there are no excluded. For Christians everybody is under the rainbow of love of the Father. Under this light, those who are distant become closer; and those who are closer to us become our brothers and sisters.

The New Covenant of Blood

The God of Christianity is a God that is embodied in all suffering and who has come down to us on two levels. He came down to us when he became man; and as man he came down again when he became poor, oppressed and enslaved, and thus, part of the weakest portion of humankind.

Throughout history God found himself wherever people did not have the sufficient means to support themselves, wherever people suffered injustices that dehumanized them, where people were unjustly crucified. These are not the sole places to meet God, but they are very important for God. If they are forgotten, then meeting God in other places becomes problematic. Jon Sobrino, the theologian from El Salvador, who was a friend and assistant of the martyr Dom Oscar Arnulfo Romero (both of whom had their lives so many times threatened) always reminded us of this in his writings in a very moving way. Therefore, God accepted the different, and moreover, he accepted the most different, that is, he accepted the sinner. I paraphrase the strong words of Paul when I say that Jesus became flesh of the sin (cf. Romans 8:3).

God forged a covenant with the different. God did not see the different as a threat, as a competitor and as an enemy that must be defeated, like we, Westerners, do. God made the different an ally in his plan for the world and in his rescue of creation. With Christ, God definitely confirmed his covenant with us. It is for this very reason that in Christ we find neither chauvinism or feminism, nor do we find the Arab, the Turk, the Black, the White; rather, we find that we are all the same community of brothers and sisters, who are citizens of the world.

Christ did not forge this new covenant with words; he forged it with his own blood. This very blood continues to be spilled nowadays as the blood of the Turks who are killed by radical racists in Germany; as the blood of the street kids who are murdered in so many Brazilian and South American cities; as the blood of the Ianomani Indians of the Amazon, who are threatened with extermination by gold prospectors and by the policy of integration of the Brazilian Government.

This atrocious reality constitutes a challenge to our faith in the eternal covenant with Jesus. A great bishop of the Brazilian Amazon region, Dom Pedro Casaldáliga, confessed with immense sorrow that: "Sometimes, I feel that the disappearance of entire nations is a strange mystery of historical injustice that weakens my faith."

Let us transform this covenant of blood into an alternative political attitude that encompasses those who are different from us; exactly because, today, we are being called to live a universal kind of citizenship and to help create a global democracy.

The Power of Small Things

Certainly, many people will say: we are so few; how are we to change the world? How are we to put into practice these small changes? Christianity has only one answer to these questions. There is a hidden power within small things, and to tap into this power one must be committed to truth. Israel, "the smallest nation on Earth" (Deuteronomy 7:7), was the first to signal us with redemption. The liberating Messiah was "despised...rejected... ignored...as if he was nothing" (Isaiah 53:3). Nonetheless, it was through him that, according to Christian belief, a new meaning of life was established. We must believe in the revolutionary powers of the small seeds. Changes in our hearts, the rise of a new benevolent and global consciousness, our small revolutions, the dream of a global social democracy – all these things are pointing the way to a new era for all humankind.

This will only happen, however, if we become utterly convinced of the rightfulness of this cause and if we persevere in it continuously. Mao Tsé-tung once said that: "we will only do the ten thousand steps trip if we have the courage to take the first step."

A weak man plus another weak man do not add up to two weak men, but to a strong man, because the union makes us strong.

11 Conclusion to Part II: We are All Eagles

When I was a student I heard a little story that may be understood as a metaphor for our current situation. I wrote a book about it, *A Águia e a Galinha (The Eagle and the Chicken)*. This book aimed at recovering the self-love and self-confidence of those human beings who are humiliated and to reinforce the idea that we are part of an infinite project. I want to refer to it now as a way to finish this book.

On one occasion, a peasant captured the chick of an eagle. He raised it at home with his chickens. On the surface, the eagle became like a chicken. One day the peasant received a visit from a natural scientist that knew eagles well. This scientist said: "This one is not a chicken, it is an eagle; and eagles do not scratch the ground as chickens do; eagles like to fly very high, they like to be above the mountains." The peasant replied: "But the eagle has become a chicken; it will not fly." The scientist said to him: "It does not fly at the moment, but inside itself it looks for the sun and it craves the heights; it will fly." One morning, the pair set out for the top of a mountain very early in the morning. The sun was rising. The scientist firmly held the eagle facing the sun. And then, he let it go. And the eagle, which had been transformed into a chicken, realized that it was an eagle. It flew. Its flight was wobbly at the beginning; then it became steadier. It flew higher and higher until it disappeared in the infinity of the morning sky.

My friends in dream and in hope: inside each of us there is an eagle. Our culture and the system have transformed us into chickens that only scratch the ground. But we have inside us the vocation to fly to the heights, to the infinite. Let us liberate the eagle that is hidden inside us. We must not allow ourselves to be condemned to a state of mediocrity. Let us do the flight of liberation. And let us take others with us, because we all have a hidden eagle inside us. We are all eagles.

Part III
Conclusion

12 Recreating a Utopic Horizon

We are at the end of the political and spiritual stagnation that came about with the breakdown in expectation and hopes associated with the socialist ideals and with the culture of acceptance of the status quo that is linked to global capitalism. Capitalism has not solved any of the problems that were left by that supposedly socialist project (the real socialism is something that remains a project for the future). On the contrary, the situation has worsened worldwide. Left to its own devices, and without an opposition or alternative, the hegemony of capitalism has dramatized even more the situation of the poor around the world. The acceleration of the process of accumulation has made the poor even poorer. Even worse, the poor have less hope than before. The quality of life of the rich has also suffered due to their consumerism.

Capitalism now has no excuses. It cannot hide any more its voracity and its perverse face, and as such, it cannot serve any more as a pretext for fighting socialism and stopping the communist ideals. It is eating away its two central pillars, namely, nature and the workforce. Nature faces a barbaric plundering. Workforce, after centuries of exploitation, is being made redundant in the name of new information and automation technologies without proper compensation.

Only those who are short sighted believe that the market economy is the solution to the main problems of humankind and that neo-liberalism is the final political stance of humanity. The conviction that Christianity can be revitalized through the standardization of doctrines and speech is naïve. In fact, in this light, Christianity appears even more Western and as such it is not fit to have a global perspective of humanity. These strategies only reinforce the culture of disillusion, resignation, and hopelessness.

This situation is changing, however. We are noticing on a worldwide scale small changes everywhere, which indicate that this stagnation is giving way. The waves are back to normal and the overflowed river is back to its usual level. Slowly a new hope is arising. Politicians from popular background, sons and daughters of poor families, are becoming heads of states. This fact opens up new hopes based on social policies that are directly centered in combating poverty and social exclusion.

The prospect for hope that is emerging brings with it a new level of consciousness, which sits on a new kind of experience. We are experiencing that a new kind of world is possible. We, human beings, are members of a great family; a family that is not only human, but that also includes the Earth-system with all its beings. Moreover, the cosmos is also our extended family; we all form an enormous socio-cosmic community. The stars are our sisters and the chemical elements that compose all beings are our brothers.

Despite all the problems we have faced and will face in the future, we, as a community of all things, have a common destiny. For this reason the global consciousness based on co-responsibility for the existence and life of all things is on the increase. Everything that exists and lives deserves to exist and live; after all, the vast majority of beings existed before human beings appeared. Every being has a right to have a future and to the ecological conditions that safeguard this future.

Everything new starts as an idea in the mind. The ideas of a global civilization and of a citizenship of the Earth have been manifesting themselves in such a way for some time. There is the rise of blocs, economies have grouped themselves in continental unions, and increasingly we see new organisms appearing in the world, organisms whose policies are aimed at the development of humanity. These are the first signs of a new dawn.

It is true that the current process of globalization meets with great contradictions. The idea of nation-states is still in place, while the notion of ecology has crossed all frontiers. Pollution in the Earth's atmosphere and the hole in the ozone layer are mainly caused by industrialized nations, who are also responsible for 80 percent of the world's air and water pollution. Countries and regions that are not direct neighbors of these polluting countries suffer the harmful consequences of this contamination. Societies are still holding on to those old paradigms that divide humanity in ethnic groups, classes, ideologies, religions; all these categories, however, must be relative to the wider process of globalization and to the structure of humankind as a united and diverse humanity. Cultures are becoming increasingly more inward-looking. These cultures fear that they are losing all that they have constructed throughout the centuries, and as such, they become more aggressive and self-centered. These cultures become very conservative and even reactionary, thus the great rise of fundamentalism and exclusion that we are currently seeing in various regions of the world.

The simple rationale of identity and difference does not have enough strength to safeguard cultures. Cultures must incorporate the rationale of dialogue so that they are open to other cultures, listen to their messages, learn wise lessons, and at the same time are able to witness their own interior richness. The rationale of dialogue presupposes the rationality (the Logos) of the web of all inter-relations; it presupposes the rationality that inheres in the inter-retro-relations with all and for all. This rationality is suitable to the complexities of reality as it enables us to identify opposites and even the contradictory as being complementing features within the great system of life and of humanity. It is through this rationality that we can put a stop to the particular that is strong and that tries to impose itself as universal. The universal can only be achieved through the union of particulars that respect each other, appreciate each other, engage in dialogue, and learn together and put themselves to the service of the mysteries of life and of the world. This rationality brings about all the points in common that the particulars have, and in so doing it helps them to walk side by side, respecting their differences, which are no longer understood as inequalities.

Despite the contradictions, the reality of globalization and of a higher level of a collective consciousness is unavoidable. Those who point out the contradictions in order to question this new reality are right about the contradictions, but they must not forget that this new reality is emerging. The realism of the brutality of the facts is not sufficiently realist because within reality we also find the potential and the ideal, which are dimensions of the whole of reality that are still not realized. Crude reality condemns us to fatalism, resignation, and to hopelessness. The potential and the ideal, as dimensions, and not as contradictions, of the whole of reality open up perspectives for the future and construct a new prospect of ideals that creates building forces that are embracing of the new and of the non-tried.

My meditation on these issues is aimed at encouraging the debate on the prospect of these new ideals. We can be sure that new perspectives will arise during and after this current crisis. I refer back to the analogy used previously. The important thing is to give wings to the eagle so that it can take off and reach the heights. The eagle must face the sun and have some hope hidden within itself.

Fernando Pessoa rightly noted that: "we must measure ourselves by the size of things we are able to see and not of the measure of our own size." Our size is of a small being, miniscule, that is lost within the infinite dimensions of the universe. But we are able to see beyond the limits of the universe and feel the heartbeat of the other and of God himself. We are in a valley, but we guide ourselves by the top of the mountains and by the stars. We can unite the abyss with the stars. For this reason we can wait for a time with no contradictions. This is the aim of my current meditations.

Appendix A: Earth's Charter[1]

Preamble

We stand at a critical moment in the Earth's history, a time when humanity must choose its future. As the world becomes increasingly interdependent and fragile, the future at once holds great peril and great promise. To move forward we must recognize that in the midst of a magnificent diversity of cultures and life forms we are one human family and one Earth community with a common destiny. We must join together to bring forth a sustainable global society founded on respect for nature, universal human rights, economic justice, and a culture of peace. Towards this end, it is imperative that we, the peoples of Earth, declare our responsibility to one another, to the greater community of life, and to future generations.

Earth, Our Home

Humanity is part of a vast evolving universe. Earth, our home, is alive with a unique community of life. The forces of nature make existence a demanding and uncertain adventure, but Earth has provided the conditions essential to life's evolution. The resilience of the community of life and the well-being of humanity depend upon preserving a healthy biosphere with all its ecological systems, a rich variety of plants and animals, fertile soils, pure waters, and clean air. The global environment with its finite resources is a common concern of all peoples. The protection of Earth's vitality, diversity, and beauty is a sacred trust.

The Global Situation

The dominant patterns of production and consumption are causing environmental devastation, the depletion of resources, and a massive extinction of species. Communities are being undermined. The benefits of development are not shared equitably and the gap between rich and poor is widening. Injustice, poverty, ignorance, and violent conflict are widespread and the cause of great suffering. An unprecedented rise in human population has overburdened ecological and social systems. The foundations of global security are threatened. These trends are perilous – but not inevitable.

The Challenges Ahead

The choice is ours: form a global partnership to care for Earth and one another or risk the destruction of ourselves and the diversity of life. Fundamental changes are needed in our values, institutions, and ways of living. We must realize that when basic needs have been met, human development is primarily about being more, not having more. We have the knowledge and technology to provide for all and to reduce our impacts on the environment. The emergence of a global civil society is creating new opportunities to build a democratic and humane world. Our environmental, economic, political, social, and spiritual challenges are interconnected, and together we can forge inclusive solutions.

Universal Responsibility

To realize these aspirations, we must decide to live with a sense of universal responsibility, identifying ourselves with the whole Earth community as well as our local communities.

We are at once citizens of different nations and of one world in which the local and global are linked. Everyone shares responsibility for the present and future well-being of the human family and the larger living world. The spirit of human solidarity and kinship with all life is strengthened when we live with reverence for the mystery of being, gratitude for the gift of life, and humility regarding the human place in nature.

We urgently need a shared vision of basic values to provide an ethical foundation for the emerging world community. Therefore, together in hope we affirm the following interdependent principles for a sustainable way of life as a common standard by which the conduct of all individuals, organizations, businesses, governments, and transnational institutions is to be guided and assessed.

Principles

I. RESPECT AND CARE FOR THE COMMUNITY OF LIFE

1. **Respect Earth and life in all its diversity.**
   a. Recognize that all beings are interdependent and every form of life has value regardless of its worth to human beings.
   b. Affirm faith in the inherent dignity of all human beings and in the intellectual, artistic, ethical, and spiritual potential of humanity.

2. **Care for the community of life with understanding, compassion, and love.**
   a. Accept that with the right to own, manage, and use natural resources comes the duty to prevent environmental harm and to protect the rights of people.
   b. Affirm that with increased freedom, knowledge, and power comes increased responsibility to promote the common good.

3. **Build democratic societies that are just, participatory, sustainable, and peaceful.**
   a. Ensure that communities at all levels guarantee human rights and fundamental freedoms and provide everyone with an opportunity to realize his or her full potential.
   b. Promote social and economic justice, enabling all to achieve a secure and meaningful livelihood that is ecologically responsible.

4. **Secure Earth's bounty and beauty for present and future generations.**
   a. Recognize that the freedom of action of each generation is qualified by the needs of future generations.
   b. Transmit to future generations values, traditions, and institutions that support the long-term flourishing of Earth's human and ecological communities.

In order to fulfill these four broad commitments, the following is necessary:

II. ECOLOGICAL INTEGRITY

5. **Protect and restore the integrity of Earth's ecological systems, with special concern for biological diversity and the natural processes that sustain life.**
   a. Adopt at all levels sustainable development plans and regulations that make environmental conservation and rehabilitation integral to all development initiatives.
   b. Establish and safeguard viable nature and biosphere reserves, including wild lands and marine areas, to protect Earth's life support systems, maintain biodiversity, and preserve our natural heritage.
   c. Promote the recovery of endangered species and ecosystems.
   d. Control and eradicate non-native or genetically modified organisms harmful to native species and the environment, and prevent the introduction of such harmful organisms.
   e. Manage the use of renewable resources such as water, soil, forest products, and marine life in ways that do not exceed rates of regeneration and that protect the health of ecosystems.

f. Manage the extraction and use of non-renewable resources such as minerals and fossil fuels in ways that minimize depletion and cause no serious environmental damage.

6. **Prevent harm as the best method of environmental protection and, when knowledge is limited, apply a precautionary approach.**
a. Take action to avoid the possibility of serious or irreversible environmental harm even when scientific knowledge is incomplete or inconclusive.
b. Place the burden of proof on those who argue that a proposed activity will not cause significant harm, and make the responsible parties liable for environmental harm.
c. Ensure that decision-making addresses the cumulative, long-term, indirect, long distance, and global consequences of human activities.
d. Prevent pollution of any part of the environment and allow no build-up of radioactive, toxic, or other hazardous substances.
e. Avoid military activities damaging to the environment.

7. **Adopt patterns of production, consumption, and reproduction that safeguard Earth's regenerative capacities, human rights, and community well-being.**
a. Reduce, reuse, and recycle the materials used in production and consumption systems, and ensure that residual waste can be assimilated by ecological systems.
b. Act with restraint and efficiency when using energy, and rely increasingly on renewable energy sources such as solar and wind.
c. Promote the development, adoption, and equitable transfer of environmentally sound technologies.
d. Internalize the full environmental and social costs of goods and services in the selling price, and enable consumers to identify products that meet the highest social and environmental standards.
e. Ensure universal access to healthcare that fosters reproductive health and responsible reproduction.
f. Adopt lifestyles that emphasize the quality of life and material sufficiency in a finite world.

8. **Advance the study of ecological sustainability and promote the open exchange and wide application of the knowledge acquired.**
a. Support international scientific and technical cooperation on sustainability, with special attention to the needs of developing nations.
b. Recognize and preserve the traditional knowledge and spiritual wisdom in all cultures that contribute to environmental protection and human well-being.

c. Ensure that information of vital importance to human health and environmental protection, including genetic information, remains available in the public domain.

III. SOCIAL AND ECONOMIC JUSTICE

9. **Eradicate poverty as an ethical, social, and environmental imperative.**
   a. Guarantee the right to potable water, clean air, food, security, uncontaminated soil, shelter, and safe sanitation, allocating the national and international resources required.
   b. Empower every human being with the education and resources to secure a sustainable livelihood, and provide social security and safety nets for those who are unable to support themselves.
   c. Recognize the ignored, protect the vulnerable, serve those who suffer, and enable them to develop their capacities and to pursue their aspirations.

10. **Ensure that economic activities and institutions at all levels promote human development in an equitable and sustainable manner.**
    a. Promote the equitable distribution of wealth within nations and among nations.
    b. Enhance the intellectual, financial, technical, and social resources of developing nations, and relieve them of onerous international debt.
    c. Ensure that all trade supports sustainable resource use, environmental protection, and progressive labor standards.
    d. Require multinational corporations and international financial organizations to act transparently in the public good, and hold them accountable for the consequences of their activities.

11. **Affirm gender equality and equity as prerequisites to sustainable development and ensure universal access to education, healthcare, and economic opportunity.**
    a. Secure the human rights of women and girls and end all violence against them.
    b. Promote the active participation of women in all aspects of economic, political, civil, social, and cultural life as full and equal partners, decision-makers, leaders, and beneficiaries.
    c. Strengthen families and ensure the safety and loving nurture of all family members.

12. **Uphold the right of all, without discrimination, to a natural and social environment supportive of human dignity, bodily health, and spiritual well-being, with special attention to the rights of indigenous peoples and minorities.**

   a. Eliminate discrimination in all its forms, such as that based on race, color, sex, sexual orientation, religion, language, and national, ethnic or social origin.

   b. Affirm the right of indigenous peoples to their spirituality, knowledge, lands and resources and to their related practice of sustainable livelihoods.

   c. Honor and support the young people of our communities, enabling them to fulfill their essential role in creating sustainable societies.

   d. Protect and restore outstanding places of cultural and spiritual significance.

IV. DEMOCRACY, NONVIOLENCE, AND PEACE

13. **Strengthen democratic institutions at all levels, and provide transparency and accountability in governance, inclusive participation in decision-making, and access to justice.**

   a. Uphold the right of everyone to receive clear and timely information on environmental matters and all development plans and activities which are likely to affect them or in which they have an interest.

   b. Support local, regional and global civil society, and promote the meaningful participation of all interested individuals and organizations in decision-making.

   c. Protect the rights to freedom of opinion, expression, peaceful assembly, association, and dissent.

   d. Institute effective and efficient access to administrative and independent judicial procedures, including remedies and redress for environmental harm and the threat of such harm.

   e. Eliminate corruption in all public and private institutions.

   f. Strengthen local communities, enabling them to care for their environments, and assign environmental responsibilities to the levels of government where they can be carried out most effectively.

14. **Integrate into formal education and life-long learning the knowledge, values, and skills needed for a sustainable way of life.**

   a. Provide all, especially children and youth, with educational opportunities that empower them to contribute actively to sustainable development.

   b. Promote the contribution of the arts and humanities as well as the sciences in sustainability education.

    c. Enhance the role of the mass media in raising awareness of ecological and social challenges.

    d. Recognize the importance of moral and spiritual education for sustainable living.

15. **Treat all living beings with respect and consideration.**

    a. Prevent cruelty to animals kept in human societies and protect them from suffering.

    b. Protect wild animals from methods of hunting, trapping, and fishing that cause extreme, prolonged, or avoidable suffering.

    c. Avoid or eliminate to the full extent possible the taking or destruction of non-targeted species.

16. **Promote a culture of tolerance, nonviolence, and peace.**

    a. Encourage and support mutual understanding, solidarity, and cooperation among all peoples and within and among nations.

    b. Implement comprehensive strategies to prevent violent conflict and use collaborative problem-solving to manage and resolve environmental conflicts and other disputes.

    c. Demilitarize national security systems to the level of a non-provocative defense posture, and convert military resources to peaceful purposes, including ecological restoration.

    d. Eliminate nuclear, biological, and toxic weapons and other weapons of mass destruction.

    e. Ensure that the use of orbital and outer space supports environmental protection and peace.

    f. Recognize that peace is the wholeness created by right relationships with oneself, other persons, other cultures, other life, Earth, and the larger whole of which all are a part.

The Way Forward

As never before in history, common destiny beckons us to seek a new beginning. Such renewal is the promise of these Earth Charter principles. To fulfill this promise, we must commit ourselves to adopt and promote the values and objectives of the Charter.

This requires a change of mind and heart. It requires a new sense of global interdependence and universal responsibility. We must imaginatively develop and apply the vision of a sustainable way of life locally, nationally, regionally, and globally. Our cultural diversity is a precious heritage and different cultures will find their own distinctive ways to realize the vision. We must deepen and expand the global dialogue that generated the Earth

Charter, for we have much to learn from the ongoing collaborative search for truth and wisdom.

Life often involves tensions between important values. This can mean difficult choices. However, we must find ways to harmonize diversity with unity, the exercise of freedom with the common good, short-term objectives with long-term goals. Every individual, family, organization, and community has a vital role to play. The arts, sciences, religions, educational institutions, media, businesses, non-governmental organizations, and governments are all called to offer creative leadership. The partnership of government, civil society, and business is essential for effective governance.

In order to build a sustainable global community, the nations of the world must renew their commitment to the United Nations, fulfill their obligations under existing international agreements, and support the implementation of Earth Charter principles with an international legally binding instrument on environment and development.

Let ours be a time remembered for the awakening of a new reverence for life, the firm resolve to achieve sustainability, the quickening of the struggle for justice and peace, and the joyful celebration of life.

Appendix B:
The Ages of Globalization*

Millions of years ago a superior primate, the *Homo sapiens-demens*, emerged in Africa. Thousands of years later, humans started spreading around the world; first to Eurasia, then to the Americas, and lastly to Polynesia and Oceania. At the end of the later Palaeolithic age, about 40,000 years ago, human beings occupied the whole of the planet and amounted to one million people. They created civilizations and nation-states.

From 1492, however, we see a vast process of expansion from the West. In 1492, Columbus brought to the knowledge of the Europeans the fact that there are other lands inhabited by cultures that are totally different from the European. In 1521, Ferdinand Magellan proved that the Earth is round and that each place can be reached from anywhere in the world. The supreme powers of the 16th century, Spain and Portugal, designed, for the first time, the world-project. They expanded into Africa, America and Asia. They Westernized the world.

This process extended into the 19th century, when Western Imperialism forced all of the known world to submit to its cultural, religious and economic interests. All of these were forced upon the weaker nations with extreme violence. Arms and canons are more powerful than rationality and religion. The Europeans revealed themselves as the hyenas of the nations. We, in the Americas, were born globalized and we know the meaning of globalization since we have experienced it, we have felt and suffered it as a global colonization.

The process had its apex in the second half of the 20th century with the expansion in the West, particularly in the USA, of the techno-science, which became a weapon of (1) domination and of wealth for the global corporations that control national markets, (2) standardization of Western cultural trends that undermines regional cultures, (3) a unique means of production, capitalism, which is founded on competition that destroys cooperation and relations in society, and (4) a single ideology, namely neo-liberal, that dominates all quarters of the Earth. The most worrying thing, however, is the fact that the process has now turned the Earth into a business area, where everything is traded and sold with profit in mind. There is no respect for the autonomy and subjectivity of Gaia. People do not realize that they have their roots and origins in the Earth; we came from the earth, from the humus, from the fertile soil, as sons and daughters of Adam, who himself came from the earth, from the Adamah, from the rich soil.

The Tyrannosauric Age of Globalization

I call this age tyrannosauric because its violence is analogous to the aggression of the tyrannosaurus, the most voracious of the dinosaurs. In fact, the rationality of competition, without any concern for cooperation, ascribes traces of cruelty to the current process of globalization. It excludes about half of humankind. It drains the economies of weak and undeveloped countries of resources, and this cruelty condemns millions and millions to starvation and malnutrition. It is so ecologically demanding that it threatens the whole biosphere; it pollutes the air, it poisons the soil, it contaminates the water and it taints the food with toxic substances. Nothing stops the tyrannosauric voracity of this age, not even the real possibility that it may make the whole global-human project impossible. It prefers death to the reduction of its own material benefits. The French geneticist Albert Jaquard noted well that: "The purpose of society is exchange. A society that is centered in competition is a society that leads me to suicide. If I must compete with my fellows, then I cannot exchange with them, I must eliminate them, destroy them."

This model of globalization based on exclusion may split the human family in two. On the one hand there will be a small group of opulent nations that will be enriching themselves in material consumption along with a deficiency in their spiritual and humanitarian values; these nations will put all the benefits of techo-science to their service. On the other hand there will be those millions living in barbaric conditions, left to their own devices, mere cogwheels in the capitalist machine, condemned to die before their time, victims of famines, of the diseases of the poor and of the degradation of the Earth. There are a number of reasons for opposing this kind of globalization. It cannot be allowed to progress as it will jeopardize the very future of the human species.

The Human Age of Globalization

The tyrannosauric age, despite all of its contradictions, brings with it an important contribution to the process of globalization when this is seen from a different perspective. It creates the infrastructural and material conditions for the other kinds of globalization. It created the great avenues of global communication, the means of commercial and financial exchange, increased exchange between people, continents and nations. Without all these pre-conditions it would have been impossible to dream of new kinds of globalization. These other kinds have always been in the background of economic globalization, and have never achieved supremacy.

Now that economic globalization is well established, human globalization must utilize its gains within the wider scenario – a scenario that encompasses all – and seek to achieve supremacy. This human globalization takes place on various fronts, such as anthropology, politics, ethics and spirituality, simultaneously. Let us enquire into these.

It is increasingly more evident to the collective consciousness that the human species is one, *sapiens* and *demens*. Despite cultural differences, we all share the same basic genetic makeup, have the same anatomic constitution, the same psychological mechanisms, the same spiritual impulses, the same archetypal desires. We all have the capacity for emotion, rationality, freedom, creativity, benevolence, love, play, wit, music, artistic expression and spiritual experience – only the ways that these are expressed are different. Simultaneously, there is also the manifestation of our capacity for pettiness, exclusion of the other, violence against nature, destruction, vengeance, and death. We are the unity of these two opposite forces.

We increasingly see the conviction that each person is sacred (i.e. *res sacra homo*). This conviction emerged in the West, but it is not Western, it is human; it is an end in itself, and as such it can never be a means to something else. This conviction is an endless project; it is the visible side of the mystery of the world; each person is a son and daughter of God. Founded on this principle is the foundation of basic human, personal and social rights. Further developments of these rights are the rights of nations, minorities, women, children, the elderly, and the sick. Lastly, there is the elaboration of the *dignitas terra*, which is the ascription of rights to the Earth as a supra-organism that is alive, to the ecosystems, to animals and to everything that exists and is alive.

Democracy as a universal value that must be lived in all spheres of human life is being slowly incorporated by the various world political stances. It is noteworthy that each human being has a right to participate in the society that he or she helps create by taking part in it and also through his or her labor. Power must be controlled so that it does not become tyrannical. Violence is not the path to long-lasting solutions; rather, vigorous dialogue, incessant tolerance and the permanent search for unions in diversities are needed. Peace is simultaneously a method (i.e. the continual use of peaceful means or means that are the least destructive possible) and a goal; it is the fruit of concerns of all for all, for the common house we live in and for undeniable concern for social justice. All institutions must become fair, egalitarian and transparent.

A minimal consensus for a global ethic is found in the humanity, *humanitas*, that each and all of us carry within us. More than a mere concept humanity, *humanitas*, is at last a deep feeling that we are brothers and sisters; we share the same origins, we have the same physic-chemical-bio-socio-cultural-spiritual nature and we share the same destiny. We must *humanly* treat everybody, following the golden rule: "Do not do to others what you do not wish done to you."

Reverence for life, a deep respect for innocents, preservation of the physical and psychological integrity of all human beings and of the whole of creation – all acknowledge that others have the right to exist as well as to choose the way they live their lives – all these constitute the basic pillars of human sociability, the values and the meaning of our short sojourn on this planet.

Spiritual experiences from the East and West, from ancient and modern cultures, are meeting each other and exchanging ideas. Through these experiences human beings are able to re-connect themselves to the original source of all life, create an unexplainable link that connects the whole universe and re-unifies all things in a totality of dynamic inter-retro-relations that drive development forward. These spiritual experiences realized in different religions and ways shape human subjectivity and recoup a wide range of perspectives that take human beings beyond this universe and to infinity. Only in this dimension of extrapolation and of overcoming limits, space and time, and desire, can human beings feel really human. The ancient Greeks taught us this lesson as they maintained that it is only within the Divine that the human being is truly human.

The human age of globalization has not yet achieved supremacy. But we can see the signs that it is flourishing as time goes by in the consciousness of people. This age will gloriously rise up one day. It will set a new chapter in the history of the human family, a family that has searched for a very long time for its common roots and for its maternal home.

The Ecozoic Age of Globalization

The term "ecozoic" was coined by two Americans, the cosmologist Brian Swimme and the anthropologist Thomas Berry, in their book *The Universe Story*. Ecozoic is the age that comes after the Cainozoic. After the catastrophe that exterminated the dinosaurs, mammals started developing themselves to levels never seen before. Human beings appeared at the apex of this Cainozoic period as a complex and advanced mammal.

We are now seeing the dawn of a new era, an era which is characterized by a new agreement aimed at respect, veneration and mutual collaboration between the Earth and humankind. This is an era of proper ecology, thus the name ecozoic. We, human beings, realized that we are a mere moment in a process that is lasting billions of years. We find ourselves in a web of vital relations and we are co-responsible for these relations. We can support life, ecosystems, and the future of Gaia; and we can also threaten Gaia, frustrate our own destiny and decimate the biosphere. After intervening so much with the rhythms of nature without caring about the awful consequences of our acts, now we realize that we must take care of everything that we can and help heal the injuries we have inflicted on nature.

We feel a kind of benevolence towards the Earth. The Earth is like a spaceship with a vast amount of resources; however, these resources are also limited. Only with the full cooperation of all can we make these resources adequate for the whole community of life. We either take care of each other and together take care of the Earth, its ecosystems and the immense biodiversity, or our future cannot be guaranteed.

This concern must encompass everybody and be the source of a new age in the process of globalization. It will mean the authentic humanization of the human being; it will mean that human beings will live as individuals in communities, cooperating with each other, with benevolence, and in an ethical manner so that they will take responsibility for their actions. Thus, all of their actions will aim at the well-being of all creation and at the common future of the Earth and humankind.

Departing from such a perspective we will design a new kind of ethical theory. Everywhere we see seminal forces trying to implement a new standard for human and ecological action. These views will force their way so that they will achieve hegemony over previous views. It will represent that which Pierre Teilhard de Chardin called *noosphere*. This is the higher level of consciousness where minds and hearts would enter into a fine connection of love, concern for each other and for a collective spiritual meaning. These would be coordinated to guarantee peace, integrity for creation and sufficient and even abundant material means for all human beings. We would be free and unburdened and as such we would be able to co-live with each other as brothers and sisters, to combine work with pleasure, efficiency with bonuses, re-connect all subjectivity, and able to play and worship as sons and daughters at home.

The understanding that we belong to both humanity and the Earth is strongly reinforced by the new perspectives that are given to us by the views of some astronauts. From their space ships or from the moon they pass to us the deep impact of their experiences. The astronaut Gene Cernan related that: "I was the last man to set foot on the moon in December 1972. From the lunar surface I looked with extreme reverence to the Earth in a deep blue background. What I saw was too beautiful to be described, it was too logical and full of purpose to be a mere cosmic accident. We felt deep inside obliged to worship God. God must exist for he created that which I was privileged to contemplate." Sigmund Jähn, another astronaut, on returning to Earth expressed his change of opinion: "Political frontiers are a thing of the past, and so are the frontiers between nations. We are a unique people and each of us is responsible for the upkeep of Earth's fragile equilibrium. We are its guardians and as such we must pursue our common future."

The perception of the Earth from outside gives rise to a new kind of sacredness. It brings with it a feeling of awe and respect. Perhaps our trips to outer space have a hidden meaning, a meaning that has been described well by the astronaut J. P. Allen: "There was a lot of arguments regarding the pros and cons of a trip to the moon; I did not hear anyone saying that we should go to the moon so that we could see the Earth from there; at any rate, this was the true reason for us going to the moon."

From the moon there is no distinction between the Earth and humankind. Both form the same entity. Nor is humankind set over and apart from the Earth, as I have said on other occasions; it *is* the Earth insofar as the Earth feels, reflects on itself, loves, takes care and worships.

If we are able to transform this understanding in a permanent state of mind, a state in which we do not need to think about it, then this will mean that we are living in the ecozoic era. We need to evolve greatly if we are to achieve this level of collective consciousness. The first steps have been taken, however. With a few more steps this understanding will be able to be part of our consciousness, and this will take us to a higher level.

The Earth Charter (i.e. a document that is the outcome of almost ten years of work by representatives from all continents and which aims to be accepted by the United Nations and so have the same status as that of the Human Rights Charters) is deeply influenced by ecozoic views. In its introduction it states that:

> Humanity is part of a vast evolving universe. Earth, our home, is alive with a unique community of life… The spirit of human solidarity and kinship with all life is strengthened when we live with reverence for the mystery of being, gratitude for the gift of life, and humility regarding the human place in nature… Our environmental, economic, political, social, and spiritual challenges are interconnected, and together we can forge inclusive solutions… The choice is ours: form a global partnership to care for Earth and one another or risk the destruction of ourselves and the diversity of life. Fundamental changes are needed in our values, institutions, and ways of living.

Despite the hindering obstacles that the tyrannosauric age brings, these necessary changes are occurring in the very heart of humanity, they are occurring in the young, students, workers, technicians, researchers, and religious people; they are occurring in so many men and women who feel they are chained to a paradigm that dehumanizes them and destroys blessed horizons, and as such, these men and women seek to implement small changes, changes in themselves that radiate throughout the whole of society.

In order to facilitate the rise and consolidation of this human and ecozoic globalization we must develop some basic virtues, which are linked to hospitality and to co-living with the other, the different and the strange. The exile is over. All the tribes of the Earth find themselves in the great common village, in the common house, and in the bosom of the great and generous mother Earth.[1]

Appendix C: The Globalization Process and its Challenges to Liberation Theology*

One of the particularities of liberation theology rests on its methodology. (1) It departs from an historical-social reality; (2) it is viewed from the perspective of the victimized; (3) it is then enlightened by the Christian faith; (4) in so doing, it aims at bringing about changes, that is; (5) it aims at rescuing the poor and the oppressed by means of a society that is politically more participative, economically more inclusive, culturally more pluralist and religiously more ecumenical.

What kind of challenges does the process of globalization pose to the kind of religious thinking that emerged in the Third World in the 1970s and that has been embraced worldwide by the ecumenical community?

Let us first enquire into the phenomena of globalization. After this is done, let us identify some challenges to Liberation Theology.

Globalization: A Trend in Anthropogenesis

We are now used to seeing the cosmos as a cosmogenesis, anthropology as anthropogenesis. The human being has been in a process of development for millions of years and this process is not finished yet. There is a tendency in human beings to expand themselves to all corners of the Earth. For this reason human beings were able to adapt themselves to all ecosystems, from the glaciers of Antarctica to the torrid deserts of the Sahara. This is the biological triumph of the species *homo*. Globalization is present in this tendency that human beings have always possessed. It became a tangible project, however, in the 16th century when the European culture expanded itself to all quarters of the world. It created the world-project. This desire for globalization was made technically possible when in 1521 Ferdinand Magellan circumnavigated the Earth. From the 16th century to the present we have experienced the Westernization of the world. Western culture has managed to impose on all peoples the way it approaches nature by using techno-science, the manner society is organized (i.e. representative democracy), the concept it has of what constitutes a person (i.e. a citizen with absolute rights), and the manner by which it understands and worships God (i.e. Christianity as the supreme religion in the world).

   This process occurred with great violence. The worst ethnocide in human history occurred during the invasion of Mexico and Peru – 24 out of 25 native Indians died within 70 years. Africa was colonized and totally destabilized. The Eastern nations felt the might of the military and economic power of the West. Wonderful spiritual traditions were weakened by the European cultural and religious influence. This is what I call the tyrannosauric age of globalization. This age, however, has created the foundations for the process of globalization that is currently greatly accelerating and diversifying. The process is occurring in three main areas, namely, the economy, politics and spirituality.

Globalization through a Global Market Economy

Globalization primarily occurs through the economy. The economy of all countries is inter-dependent, that is, the regional markets have integrated themselves in the world market. Three factors characterize this globalization through economics.

   The first characteristic is the advent of mega-conglomerates and strategic corporations that act on a global level. These are no more trans-national companies; rather, these are world firms. Mitsubishi, which has a Japanese base, is an example of this; it is present worldwide and it has interests in 90 different areas. There are other examples of this, such as Daimler-Benz and Ciba-Geygy. Great conglomerates work in global partnerships, such as Ford (USA) with Mazda (Japan), General Motors with Isuzu, Fiat with Nissan, and so on. These conglomerates act on a global level consonant with market economics and searching for profitable advantages – many times this is done with no state supervision.

   Secondly, we find the grouping of economies in continental unions; this is done within the wider process of globalization. Instances of this are the European Union, NAFTA (USA, Canada and Mexico), Asian tigers, and Mercosul (Brazil, Argentina, Uruguay and Paraguay). There is a real economic war between these economic blocks. The competition between these blocs causes great technological advances and at the same time aggravates the ecological crises and widens the gap between the technologically advanced and underdeveloped countries.

   The third characteristic is the rise of trans-national elites that set out to manage the world's politics and economics; in doing so, these elites make the role of the state and national interests relative. Such facts compel us to rethink the role of the nation-states and to understand the need for a global government that articulates the basic collective interests of the Earth as a whole and of humanity as a species.

Globalization through Politics

Along with globalization through economics comes globalization through politics. Because of Western influences, practically all peoples have organized themselves in nation-states. The idea of democracy has penetrated the political habits of all countries; be it democracy as a universal value that ought to be lived in human relationships in schools, in the community, in the productive processes, or be it democracy as a way of organizing the state itself. Democracy only functions properly when an atmosphere of respect and the promotion of personal and collective human rights are well established. Human rights presuppose, in turn, an understanding of human beings as an end in themselves and never as a means (i.e. the enduring ethical contribution of Kant), and this is not easily understood by the Eastern nations. Because of this anthropological fact and of the universal validity of human rights, all power requires constitutional demarcations and control by either the people or their representatives if it is to be considered legitimate. The World Wars and especially the Gulf War in 1991 showed the other side of globalization. In the Gulf War all nations had to position themselves one way or another; all nations became involved, globalized, behind the current supreme super power, the United States of America.

In the last few years, three issues have made the process of globalization very obvious because they impinge on all of us without exception. These are: communications, nuclear danger, and ecological warnings. (1) Communications make neighbors of us and reveal to us the unity, and diversity, of the human species. Humanity will never be the same again after the mass media. (2) Nuclear and chemical weapons are able to destroy humankind many times and dangerously threaten the biosphere. There will not be a Noah's Ark to save some, leaving others to perish. All human beings may perish as the outcome of the use of these weapons. (3) Ecological warnings were given in 1972 by the Club of Rome. The report by the Club, which has many unclear aspects, maintains an incontestable truth: the kind of technical and industrial development that has been adopted by the world implicates a systematic aggression towards nature, the exhaustion of non-renewable natural resources and the degradation of quality of life for all beings. The greenhouse effect, the poisoning of the soil and of the air, the hole in the ozone layer, can cause irreversible damage to the biosphere. Death can be brought about by ecocide (i.e. the death of ecosystems), biocide (i.e. the death of species) and geocide (i.e. the death of the Earth-Gaia).

Globalization through Spirituality

The economic and political-ecological factors discussed above brought about another factor in the process of globalization, namely, the new global consciousness. We are co-responsible for our common destiny, the common destiny of human beings and the Earth. In fact, human beings and the Earth form a single entity. For the first time in the history of anthropogenesis we are able to see the Earth from outside. This is the view that the astronauts have, a view that changes consciousnesses. The astronaut Russell Scheickhart, on returning to Earth, noticed a change in his manner of thinking. He said: "Viewed from outside the Earth is so small and fragile; it is a small and precious blot that could be covered with your thumb. Everything that has a meaning for you, history, art, being born, death, love, happiness and tears, all these things are inside that small blue and white dot that could be covered by your thumb. Once you experience this, you feel that everything has changed; you have experienced something new and things will not be as they were before."

Human beings are not mere inhabitants of the Earth. They are Earth (humus-homo-human).[1] As the Argentine poet and singer Atauhalpa Yupanqui says, a human being is the Earth that walks, thinks, speaks and loves. Stones, mountains, oceans, forests, animals and human beings are not mere parts of a whole. Everything is interlinked and organically connected. If life and matter were opposites, then we would have on one side the physical and mechanical world and on the other a biological world, and within this latter the human realm – and all these different realms would be separated by barriers that could not be breached. Matter cannot be seen as something that is static; rather, it must be seen as something that is characterized by activity, creativity and information. Life has risen from the Earth. And human life has risen from within the history of life itself. This view is being divulged worldwide by modern cosmologists. It helps us understand that the universe is an immense process of evolution that has been occurring for 15 billion years. This process is unique, complex, contradictory (chaotic and harmonious), and complementary; it unites all beings in a web of relations so that nothing can exist outside these. The passage of time shows us a particular trend; it shows us that as time goes by, more complex, auto-organized, subjective, and unified forms of life and of creative expression appear. A grasp of these issues provides the scientific and experimental basis to understand the current process of globalization as a moment in an infinitely larger process that has been occurring since the beginnings of the universe; a process that merges energies, subjectivities and activities. All these issues help explain the current process of globalization. In turn it appears, as Teilhard de Chardin would say, that the current process would provide the conditions for a qualitative jump that will lead us to a noogenesis and a noosphere, that is the genesis and the sphere of spirituality. According to this hypothesis, there will be a unity of human beings in a higher level, a unity of their minds, of their spirits, and of their hearts, and this would give rise to a new chapter in the history of the universe and in the history of human beings themselves, who would turn into more benevolent and fraternal beings.

This understanding of the process that is slowly finding its way around the world also brings with it a new spirituality. By spirituality I do not mean a religious attitude; rather, I mean a human attitude of respect and awe towards the grandiosity and magnificence of the universe and an admiration towards the complexity of life on Earth. Human beings realize that they can grasp the significance of all things because each thing is the outcome of a very long process; and human beings will also realize that they can dialogue with their inner selves and with the energies, archetypes and passions that emerge there, and in doing so they implement a process that brings with it peace and a tranquil life. For religious people the inner self is inhabited by God and to dialogue with the inner self is to be able to hear the Word of God. We increasingly see around the world a great thirst for spirituality, for a re-connection with the link that connects all things and all experiences and which gives meaning to life and truth to all religions.

Challenges to Latin American Liberation Theology

All theology sees the process of globalization as a sign that needs interpretation. The process must be greeted as another event in cosmogenesis and anthropogenesis. For religious people, the process is a sign of the will of God. A human being is essentially a web of relations; and, as such, the process of globalization enables human beings to fulfill this aspect of their being in a way never before seen.

Liberation theology, however, is characterized by its particular approach to all phenomena, namely, it approaches a phenomena from the perspective of the victims. Liberation Theology asks: What is the role of those who are poor and oppressed within the process of globalization? Here, a theological meditation takes on a prophetic dimension. Let us now analyze those three factors in the process of globalization, namely, economy, politics and spirituality, taking the perspective of the poor and oppressed as our departing point.

Globalization through economics occurs within the paradigm of capital. The reasoning behind this paradigm is the following: it has a preference for the accumulation of profit by the private sector and for competition and it aims to maximize opportunities. Because of this reasoning, globalization through economics excludes a large number of countries and people. Let us refer to statistics from the World Bank's World Development Report of 1993, as well as data from the United Nations Development Program of 1992. These reports establish that in the last 25 years, from 1965 to 1990, when the process of globalization started to accelerate, the world's wealth grew ten times over, while the world's population only doubled in number. During this period the portion of the world's wealth held by the rich countries rose from 68 percent to 72 percent, while the populations of these countries went from 30 percent to 23 percent of the world's population. Moreover, the portion of the world's wealth held by the top 20 percent of the richest people increased from 72 percent to 83 percent, while the portion of the world's poorest people went from 2.3 percent to 1.4 percent. This kind of globalization yields the death of 40,000 people by famine and malnutrition on a daily basis. Roger Garaudy notes that "in the South, this is the equivalent to a Hiroshima every two days."[2] Such distortions only show that the capitalist market economy is extremely unsupportive of an egalitarian society. The production process from this kind of economy is not aimed at human needs; rather, it is aimed at the needs of the market. I am not against economics; after all, economics is the central pillar of modern societies. *This kind* of market economy, however, is unacceptable since it victimizes the vast majority of human beings.

The rise in the number of people who are hungry in the world, the rise in the number of countries that find themselves excluded from the wider process because of their under-development, and the ecological crisis that threatens the Earth – all these issues make us feel obliged to change the current economics, if we are to survive. Economics must not be a process of linear and unlimited material growth; rather, it must be a social process centered in producing enough for all human beings and for all of creation. This latter view is supported by Liberation Theology.

Globalization through politics is currently represented by the standardization of political and cultural values at a global level; the benchmark for this standardization is centered on Western values, which liberation theology views with suspicion since Western values are just another event in the long history of the world. Our current challenge is to provide support for multicultural and multi-religious societies, and to respect the way these societies are socially and politically organized on the very basis of their respective cultures. A major challenge is to generate, bottom to top, ways of co-living that can be inclusive, inclusive of all, especially those who have been excluded throughout history. This can only be done if society is based on four central pillars, namely: participation, equality, respect of differences, and communion between human beings.

With regard to the process of globalization that occurs through spirituality, liberation theologians are certain that not only the oppressed, but also all humanity must be liberated. We are all currently living within a paradigm that enslaves us and that makes us rivals of nature by setting us apart from it. It is not only the poor that scream for help. The Earth also calls for help due to the systematic aggression that it suffers, aggression that is the outcome of the kind of development that goes against and not with nature.

Liberation theology encourages regaining the sacred character that the Earth once had, the rescue of spiritual traditions of oppressed cultures; cultures that usually have a veneration and respect for the Earth as the Great Mother. This approach will put a limit to modern greed and will allow for a new experience of God within the universe; such an experience will overcome the established Christian-Western dualisms of God and world, soul and body, feminine and masculine. Liberation theologians are convinced that only the kind of Christianity that breaks away from the alliances it has with the powers of this world, that moderates its Western image and that takes up the cause of the oppressed of the Earth, who amount to two-thirds of humankind, can reclaim Jesus' legacy. Only a Christianity of liberation, and not a Christianity of domination, is supportive of the process of globalization, a process that aims to unify us in our differences, a process that does not only occur in economics, politics and culture, but also in religious terms.

Notes

Chapter 1

1. *Les chemins vers une société de pleine activité et non plus de plein emploi,* Seville, September 17–18, 1992, 9.

2. José Comblin, "Sinais dos tempos no final do seculo XX," in *Varios, Vida, Clamor e Esperanca* (São Paulo: Loyola, 1992), 31–41.

3. Cf. P. Quéau, *Le Virtuel, Vertus et Vertiges* (Paris: Camp Vallon/INA, 1993), or P. Quéau, "La Revolution des Images Virtuelles," *Le Monde Diplomatique* (August 1993), 16–17.

4. Vide H. Bartoli, "L'economie multidimensionelle," *Econômica* (1992); R. Passet, *L'economie et le vivant* (Payot, 1979).

5. In Marc Luyckx, *Religions et Éthique après Prométhée. Positions éthiques des religions face à la science européenes* (Bruxelles, 1991), 26.

Chapter 2

1. *Terre-patrie* (Paris: Seuil, 1993), 18.

Chapter 3

1. Translation note. Boff refers here to the Hebrew word Adamah which refers to the red earth of Israel and to the fact that the word Adam (i.e. man in English) is a derivative of this word. He also traces the origins of the word *homen* (i.e. man in English) to the Latin word *humus*, which is 'translated in English as ground. The Portuguese original reads *Adamah-Adam, Humus-Homo-Homen.*

Chapter 5

1. Cf. Leonardo Boff, *Ecologia, Globalisacão, Espiritualidade* (São Paulo: Atica, 1993); and *Ecologia: Grito da Terra, Grito dos Pobres* (São Paulo: Atica, 1955).

2. Cf. R. Garaudy, *Avons-nousbesoin de Dieu?* (Paris: Desclée de Brower, 1933).

Chapter 6

1. Blaise Pascal, *Pensées*, ed. Léon Brunschvigg, introduction Emile Faguet (Paris and London: Ed. Lutetia, 1914), para. 72.

2. Translation note. The word "religion" has its roots in the Latin word "religare," which is often translated in English as "re-connect." In the Portuguese original text there is a subtle play of words between "religiao" and "re-ligar" that does not translate well in non-Latin languages.

Chapter 7

1. The source of this data is the United Nations Development Program (UNDP), *Human Development Report* (New York and Oxford: Oxford University Press, 1990).

Chapter 8

1. Paulo Sues, ed., *A Conquista Espiritual da America Latina* (Petrópolis: Vozes, 1992), 227.

Appendix A

1. Leonardo Boff is co-editor of the Earth's Charter and which is included in the original Portuguese edition of his book. He has kindly forwarded an English version of it to me, so that it could be included in the English version. More information about the Earth's Charter and versions of the text in various languages can be found on the website www.earthscharter.org and www.leonardoboff.com.

Appendix B

*   "The Ages of Globalization" is a previously unpublished paper by Leonardo Boff. He has kindly agreed to its inclusion in this edition.

1. Translation note. I have translated the word *taba* as village; it is a corruption of the word *tawa* of the Tupi-guarani language, a language spoken by many Brazilian native Indians; in its original form it refers to the common hut used by all inhabitants of an indigenous village. I have also translated the word *ilê* of the Yoruba Nigerian language, and which was spoken by many of the original African slaves that were brought to work on the Brazilian sugarcane plantations, and which is still spoken by many of their descendents, as house; it could be translated as house or home in English.

Appendix C

*   The paper "The Globalization Process and its Challenges to Liberation Theology" is a previously unpublished paper by Leonardo Boff. He has kindly agreed to its inclusion in this edition.

1. Translation note. In the Portuguese original text there is a play of words here. Boff traces the origin of the Portuguese word *homen*, man in English, to the Latin word *humus*, ground in English. Thus the original Portuguese reads *humus-homo-homen*.

2. *Vers une guerre de religion?* (Paris: Desclée, 1955), 7.

Bibliography and Further Reading

Berry, T., *The Dream of the Earth*. San Francisco: Sierra Club Books, 1990.

Betto, Fr. *Teilhard de Chardin: sinfonia universal*. São Paulo: Letras & Letras, 1992.

Boff, L. "Ökologie und Spiritualität." *Kosmiche Mystik, Evangelische Theologie* 5 (Munich, 1993).

—*Eine nue Erde in einer neuen Zeit – Plädoyer für eine planetarische Kultur*. Düsseldorf: Patmos, 1994.

—*Dignitas Terrae: ecologia, grito da Terra, grito dos pobres*. São Paulo: Atica, 1995.

—*Ecology and Liberation: A New Paradigm*. New York: Orbis Books, 1995.

—*A Águia e a Galinha*. Petrópolis: Vozes, 1997.

Boltzmannn, L. *Lectures on Gas Theory*. University of California Press, 1964.

—*Theoretical Physics and Philosophical Problems*. Ed. B. McGuinness. Dordrecht: Reidel, 1974.

Capra, F. *Tao of Physics*. London: Fontana, 1979.

—*The Turning Point*. London: Fontana, 1983.

Granrut, C. *La mondialization de l'economie, Eléments de synthèse*. Brussels: Commission des Communautés Européenes, 1990.

Hallman, D. G. *A Place in Creation*. Toronto: The United Church Publishing House, 1992.

Hawkings, S. *A Brief History of Time*. London: Bantam, 1998.

Hinkelhammert, F. J. "La lógica de la expulsion del Mercado capitalista mundial y el proyecto de liberación." *Pasos* (San José de Costa Rica), 1992.

Houtart, F. A. "A mundializacão da economia." *Cadernos de Fé e Política* 11, 1994.

Ingelhardt, R. *Sociopolitical Change in Global Perspective: Preliminary Findings from the 1990 World Values Survey*. Institute for Social Research, University of Michigan, 1991.

Kurz, R. *Der Kollps der Modernisierung, Vom Zusammenbruch des Kasernen-Sozialismus zur Krise der Weltökonoie*. Frankfurt: Vito von Eichborn Verlag, 1991.

Lovelock, J. *Gaia*. Oxford: Oxford University Press, 1987.

—*The Ages of Gaia*. Oxford: Oxford University Press, 1988.

Lutzenberger, J. *Fim do futuro?* Porto Alegre: Editora Movimento, 1980.

Luyckcx, M. *Religions et Étiques après Prométhée*. Brussels: FAST, 1992.

Meadows, D. *Limits to Growth: A Report for the Club of Rome's Project on the Predicament of Mankind*. London: Earth Island, 1972.

Moltmann, J. "Die Erde und die Menschen." *Zum theologischen Verstandnis der Gaja-Hipotese, Evangelische Theologie* 5 (Munich, 1993).

Monod, J. *Chance and Necessity*. Trans. A. Wainhouse. New York: Knopf, 1971. (French original: *Le hasard et la nécessité*. Paris: Editions du Seuil, 1970.)

Morin, E. *Science avec Conscience*. Paris: Fayard, 1991.

—*Terre-patrie*. Paris: Seuil, 1993.

Mourão, R. *Ecologia cosmica*. São Paulo: Francisco Alves, 1992.

Pascal, B. *Pensées*, ed. Léon Brunschvigg, introduction Emile Faguet. Paris and London: Editions Lutetia, 1914.

Pasternak-Pessis, G. *Do caos à inteligencia artificial*. São Paulo: Unesp, 1992.

Petrella, R. *The Globalization of Technological Innovation*. Brussels: FAST, 1990.

Prigogine, I., and I. Stengers. *A nova alianca*. São Paulo: Companhia das Letras, 1992.

—*Entre o tempo e a eternidade*. São Paulo: Companhia das Letras, 1992.

Ribeiro, D. *The Civilizational Process*. Washington: Smithsonian Institute Press, 1968.

Robin, J. *Changer d'ère*. Paris: Seuil, 1989.

Souza, W. *O novo paradigma*. São Paulo: Cultrix, 1993.

Swimme, B., and T. Berry. *The Universe Story: From the Primordial Flaring Forth to the Ecozoic Era. A Celebration of the Unfolding of the Cosmos*. San Francisco: HarperSanFrancisco.

Teilhard de Chardin, P. *L'avenir de l'homme*. Paris: Editions du Seuil, 1963.

—*Le Phénomène humain*. Paris: Editions du Seuil, 1965.

Toffler, A. *The Third Wave*. London: Collins, 1980.

Unger, N. M. *O encantamento do humano: ecologia e espiritualidade*. São Paulo: Loyola, 1991.

Weizsäcker, F. *O tempo urge*. Petropolis, Brazil: Vozes, 1991.

White, F. *The Overview Effect*. Boston: Houghton Mifflin, 1987.

Zohar, D. *The Quantum Self*. Glasgow: Flamingo, 1990.

Index of Subjects

Index of Names